Human Prehistory in Fiction

Human Prehistory in Fiction

by CHARLES DE PAOLO

McFarland & Company, Inc., Publishers
Jefferson, North Carolina, and London

Library of Congress Cataloguing-in-Publication Data

De Paolo, Charles, 1950–
    Human prehistory in fiction / by Charles De Paolo.
       p.   cm.
    Includes bibliographical references and index.

    ISBN 0-7864-1417-0 (softcover : 60# alkaline paper) ∞

    1. Fantasy literature—History and criticism.   2. Science fiction—
History and criticism.   I. Title.
PN56.F34D42   2003
809.3'876—dc21   2002151312

British Library cataloguing data are available

Manufactured in the United States of America

Cover art ©2002 Art Today and PhotoSpin

*McFarland & Company, Inc., Publishers
  Box 611, Jefferson, North Carolina 28640
   www.mcfarlandpub.com*

To my children,
Victoria and Patrick

Acknowledgments

I would like to thank my colleagues at Borough of Manhattan Community College, especially Antonio Pérez, Sadie Bragg, Erwin Wong, Phil Eggers, and Robert Zweig, for encouraging and supporting my work. I also am grateful to the college for granting my fall 2000 sabbatical leave to work on this project and for awarding me a generous faculty development grant as further support. I would also like to extend my gratitude to scholars outside the BMCC community who offered advice and insight. Special thanks are in order to David C. Smith, Arthur B. Evans, Carol McGuirk, Edward James, Farah Mendlesohn, Robert Philmus, and John S. Partington. Finally, I thank my wife, Andrea, whose technical assistance in the preparation of this manuscript I could not have done without.

Portions of this book have appeared in journals, and I would like to thank the editors for granting permission to reproduce this material here. An earlier version of chapters 5, 7, and 10 was published under the title "Wells, Golding, and Auel: Representing the Neanderthal" in *Science Fiction Studies* (November 2000); and a variant of chapter 12, entitled "*The Time Machine* and the Descent of Man," was published in *Foundation: A Review of International Science Fiction* (2002).

Contents

Abbreviations

EW.	H. G. Wells: *Early Writings in Science and Science Fiction*
DTM.	The Definitive *Time Machine*
M.Var.	*Moreau* Variorum
OED	*Oxford English Dictionary*
OH.	H. G. Wells et al.: *The Outline of History*
OTM.	Oxford *Time Machine*
SL.	*The Science of Life*

Introduction: The Problem of Authenticity

The writer of prehistoric fiction who values authenticity will be in search of what Thomas S. Kuhn calls "normal science"—a research tradition "based upon one or more past scientific achievements" that a "particular scientific community acknowledges *for a time* as supplying the foundation for its further practice" (10). I italicize the phrase *for a time* to stress one of several difficulties a writer-researcher faces when evaluating the worth of authoritative opinions. A scientific tradition such as paleoanthropology (a branch of anthropology comprising human evolution and related fields [Delson 407]) is historical and variable in nature; that is, it is *diachronic* (a term I borrow from linguistics [Wardhaugh 208]). I would therefore agree with Gerald Messadié's observation that it is not possible to declare a discovery as being definitive, since any such finding can reflect only "a part of reality" (9). To no discipline is this description more appropriate than to paleoanthropology, the history of which is a record of accumulated human fragments and of efforts to understand these discoveries fully.

An efficient approach to the study of prehistoric fiction would position a work in its intellectual context, compare it to other works of its kind, and determine whether a writer employed available scientific resources effectively. The idea of effectiveness implies that a writer is able to use current theory credibly. The ineffective use of this material, conversely, would mean that a writer either misconstrues or ignores normal science or that its incorporation interferes with characterization, theme, and other elements of fiction. The effective or ineffective use of sources can only be determined if a work of fiction is read *synchronically* (I again

1

borrow from linguistics [Wardhaugh 156, 220]), that is, in its intellectual and historical context.

Imaginative writing on human prehistory, as I have discovered, usually reflects the prevailing opinions of its scientific milieu. Whereas some writers question and test ideas critically, others may only endorse received ideas. Doctrinal fiction of this kind can be effective as well: if doctrinal science can approximate "a good theory in stages" (Popper 187), then its fictional correlative may enhance and communicate these approximations to the reader. Throughout this study, I will be dealing with the ideas of critical and of doctrinal fiction, as I analyze a writer's commitment to received authority and how this affects his or her work. The portrayals of the Neanderthal man, in 1921 (by Wells), in 1939 (by Del Rey), and in 1980 (by Auel), for example, illustrate how one's commitment to normal science may affect the fiction and represent the evidence in various ways. A synchronic approach to the fiction dealing with philosophical and cultural issues can help to account for disparate portrayals of early man.

In the preview that follows, I will show how imaginative writers interact with the body of normal science and how this interaction has produced a unique and variegated subgenre. H. G. Wells's *The Island of Doctor Moreau* rejects the biological model called the scale of nature, a traditional scheme that had become obsolete by the late nineteenth century. In this model, "the diversity of the organic world was divinely arranged as a quantitative continuum, ranging from lower to higher and more 'perfect' forms of life" (Rosenberger 504). Moreover, according to this model, all species, created through divine fiat, were thought to have been fixed and immutable.

To express his opposition to this inadequate paradigm, Wells employed the counter-myth of *heterogony* (the transmutation of one species into another). Although *The Island of Doctor Moreau* features a speciation concept more anachronistic than that which it abrogates, Wells effectively achieves his purpose: to assert the physiological affinity of man and ape (as Huxley did in 1863) and their taxonomic affiliation in the superfamily Hominoidea (which comprises man and both the lesser and greater apes [Andrews 48]).

A writer of paleoanthropological fiction may have the resources of normal science readily at hand but choose not to incorporate this material into the fiction. Pierre Boulle's *The Planet of the Apes* (1963) is a rare case in point. It contrasts with Wells's novel because Boulle exhibits neither a critical strategy nor an awareness of the considerable body of research on primate evolution and behavior of the 1960s. Fundamentally important to anyone writing imaginatively about the primate order are three crucial evolutionary events: (1) from 6.0 to 10 million years ago, the ancestor of the gorilla became differentiated from the Homininae (subfamily of the Hominoidea comprising chimpanzees, gorillas, and humans [Andrews 247]), an ancestral departure leaving the proto-ape (the forebear of the chimpanzee and man) to evolve independently and eventually to bifurcate; (2) between 3.0 and 7.0 million years ago, the chimpanzee lineage emerged from this common trunk, leaving the proto-hominid to evolve along its own trajectory; and (3), between 3.0 and 2.5 million years ago, *Australopithecus afarensis* appeared, at which point (some maintain) the human lineage began.

Despite these revelations about the primate order, available to general readers in the early 1960s, Boulle does not construct a believable parallel between Earth and his world, Soror. Failing to exploit the evolutionary possibilities of the story, he diverts his narrative into socio-political allegory and fantasy. Normal science, for Boulle, does not figure prominently in the imaginative endeavor.

The scientific orientations of Jules Verne (*The Village in the Treetops* [1901]) and of Edgar Rice Burroughs (*The Land That Time Forgot* [1924]) also contrast with Wells's thinking in *The Island of Doctor Moreau*. Both Verne and Burroughs use authentic sources, along with pseudo-science, to reinforce the arcane notion of the scale of nature. Their common strategy suggests that, as late as the early twentieth century, the scalar teleology was still viable. To create a being analogous to Eugène Dubois' missing link, Verne drew on authentic sources for his description, and many of the details suggest that he believed Dubois' creature to have been a near-human being. But he could not commit himself to this idea wholeheartedly since doing so was tantamount to rejecting the order of biblical creation in Genesis. Dubois' early human, if indeed he was human, implied that man was not specially created in the divine economy. Verne's religious commitment prevented him from humanizing this creature. He therefore debarred the Waggdis from the human family on the grounds that they had no religion, an intuition some scientists thought unique to mankind. In effect, Verne conflates paleoanthropological and pseudo-scientific elements and uses this amalgam, in turn, to support the scalar design.

Burroughs also uses normal science to support the arcane scheme. Realizing that knowledge of early man in the 1920s was fragmentary, he devised a taxonomic model (I call *phylosynthesis*) that subsumed contemporary paleontology and biogenetic theory under a pseudo-evolutionary scheme corresponding to the scale of nature. His scheme located all prehistoric forms on a progressive continuum and then transformed each form into a developmental phase in the life history of each hominid on the island of Caprona; thus, an individual could evolve from a Neanderthal, to a Cro-Magnon, to modern man, and so on. Burroughs' innovation was to enlist normal science (that is, the fossil inventory and the ideas of von Baer and of Haeckel) to support pseudo-science (the unilinear design of creation).

The effects of dubious scientific thought on the fiction of Wells (1921), of Del Rey (1939), and of Golding (1955) vary considerably from one another. The common effect is that each novel becomes a conduit for misinformation and stereotypes. Thus, the Neanderthal appears as a savage beast (in Wells), as a pathetic outcast (in Del Rey), and as an endearing imbecile (in Golding). None of these characterizations, however, had any basis in the fossil record. In Wells's "The Grisly Folk," *Homo sapiens neanderthalensis* is a man-eating beast, and the Cro-Magnon people are heroic pioneers who, in their Western European migration, are thought to have annihilated indigenous people, ca. 30,000 years ago. Wells's degradation of the Neanderthals and the annihilation theory, research would prove, were unfounded. His license, in this regard, I attribute to misinterpretation of the fossil evidence (on the part of the experts), to outright fraud, to cultural and ethnic chauvinism, and to obdurate resistance to the idea of modern man's descent from earlier creatures. These factors transform "The Grisly Folk" into an ideological document. Whereas in *The Island of Doctor Moreau* Wells criticizes received doctrine, in "The Grisly Folk" he indiscriminately embraces conservative ideology and incorrect interpretations.

Lester Del Rey's "The Day Is Done" (1939), in common with Boulle's novel, does not avail itself of thought-provoking scientific information. Once again, the sources would have benefited the fiction had they been tapped. Del Rey's story, however, is far superior to Boulle's social allegory because he creates a pathetic but dignified character in Hwoogh, the sole-surviving Neanderthal. Apparently unaware of the astounding discoveries of the early 1930s at Mount Carmel, Israel, which revealed that certain Neanderthals had modern human features and were therefore closely related genetically, Del Rey missed a dramatic opportunity. The possibility that the Neanderthals and modern man had interbred with one another would have brought greater poignancy to the story since those who marginalize and eventually murder Hwoogh would then have been identified as his genetic relatives. Under these circumstances, his death would have amounted to parricide. Clearly, the thorough investigation of source material would have enhanced the fiction had Del Rey chosen to develop the idea of genetic linkage and of the indivisible unity of the human family.

Golding's *The Inheritors* rightly criticizes the distortions promulgated in "The Grisly Folk." Although congruent with scientific authority in 1955, his hominids are as flawed as Wells's. They are artificially recast in terms the French paleontologist Marcellin Boule erroneously defined. Boule claimed to have constructed from bone fragments an anatomically correct model of the Neanderthal specimen of La Chapelle-aux-Saints. Phrenological doctrine claiming that cranial structure is an index of intelligence also influenced Golding's thinking. According to this theory, fragments of Neanderthal skulls can supply an investigator with information about the way this creature thought and behaved. With this concept in mind, Golding depicts Neanderthal consciousness in cognitively deficient terms, inferred from the shape of fossil skulls. He derived this fictional motif from the erroneous premise that a recessive forehead (typical of the Neanderthal fossil) indicates deficiencies in regions of the brain believed responsible for rational and abstract cognition. Golding's fiction, however, is inconsistent: it properly humanizes anthropoidal man; but, in relying on Boule's misconstruction and on phrenology, it reaffirms the conservative image of the Neanderthal as a benign imbecile. Golding's revision fails, ironically, because he relied on a branch of normal science (featuring Boule and the phrenologists) that modern paleoanthropology would eventually discredit.

Arthur C. Clarke's *2001: A Space Odyssey* resembles the fiction of Verne and Burroughs in the way it uses authentic (though dated) sources. The primary source for Clarke's fiction is Raymond Dart's theory of the killer-ape as man's genetic forebear. In his excavation of *Australopithecus africanus* sites in Africa, Dart theorized that this creature's tool culture consisted of bones (osteo-), of animal teeth and jaws (donto-), and of horns (keratic-). As an efficient means of describing this creature's ingenuity, he created the adjective *osteodontokeratic*. On the basis of hominid and faunal remains unearthed at Makapansgat, South Africa, he further characterized this human precursor as a predator and carnivore.

Published in 1954, his hypothesis raised two questions: is man innately violent; and, if so, is this trait inherited from *A. africanus*? Dart and his chief supporters, Robert Ardrey, Konrad Lorenz, and Desmond Morris, answered these questions affirmatively. But the South African geologist, C. K. Brain, rigorously challenged their contention, showing that *A. africanus* was more than likely the victim of predators such as the leopard than the aggressor Dart claimed him to be. One current authoritative opinion is that Dart misinterpreted the evidence.

In the novel, Clarke enacts Dart's thesis imaginatively but does not explore modern man's aggressive proclivities in terms of natural processes;

instead, he substitutes the intrusions of an alien intelligence that uses psychological conditioning to determine the human character. The use of an extra-terrestrial cause for human behavior precludes the imaginative exploration of the evolutionary forces to which humankind has been subject for millennia; specifically, the alien influence replaces random mutation as a determinant in human evolution. Clarke uses his source material well, but, in choosing an extra-terrestrial cause, contributes nothing substantive to aggressionist theory and to the debate of the 1960s.

In some works of prehistoric fiction, writers actually prefigure discoveries or achieve original insights. Inventive fiction of this kind extrapolates from natural theory or law to an imagined possibility. Chapters 9, 10, 11, and 12 feature fictional expressions ranging from the mimetic to the purely inventive. Wells's writings on the psycho-social origins of primitive religion, a topic in cultural anthropology, are indebted to an aggregate of ground-breaking theories that form the basis of our current knowledge of primitive religion. The author's success in this area of anthropology is measured in large part by the way a wide range of reputable sources is interwoven in the fiction.

Jean Auel's *The Clan of the Cave Bear* (1980), like Wells's writings on primitive religion, is a mimetic tour de force. Eschewing brutish or pristine distortions for her Neanderthals, she relies on authoritative science. In terms of language capacity, of tool technology, and of human evolutionary history, her novel is extremely credible. Unlike Wells (in 1921) and Del Rey, Auel subscribes to an extinction theory in which the Neanderthals' gene pool is assimilated into that of early-modern mankind. This intermingling of Neanderthal and of early-modern genes implies that the two subspecies had interbred for thousands of years. The theory underlying Auel's fiction reiterates the Mount Carmel hypothesis of the 1930s and, more importantly, adumbrates the 1999 discovery of the remains of a child who lived ca. 24,500 years ago, and who had both Neanderthal and early-modern anatomical features.

Anticipating the thesis that *Homo erectus* was a direct ancestor of modern man, J.-H. Rosny-Aîné in *Quest for Fire* (1911) writes inventively. A substantial amount of authentic research informs the novel. Subsequent analysis reveals Rosny's concern with the socio-cultural interrelationship between a fictive variant of *erectus* (the Oulhamrs) and collateral hominids. Rosny's narrative belongs to a 160,000 year period during which a type of *erectus* is believed to have evolved into early-modern man. Since we know very little of this transitional period, the subject is conducive to extrapolation. An enigmatic tribe of early-modern humans whose physiological anomalies destine them to extinction communicate fire technology to the Oulhamrs, literally passing the torch on to their evolutionary successors. This altruistic gesture will permit the Oulhamrs to ignite their own fires, a practice that will revolutionize their culture. The attainment of pyrotechnology will allow natural selection to work in their favor as fire brings settlement, nutritious food, better weapons, warmth, socialization, family solidarity, tribal coherence, ritual, myth, song, and legend (Toth & Schick 208). Hence, the controlled rather than the opportunistic use of fire will be the bridge to modernity which the Oulhamrs will cross as the predecessors of modern man.

In *The Time Machine* (1895), Wells extrapolates the evolutionary biology of man into the future. The use of natural acts and processes (mutation, natural selection, symbiosis, speciation, and extinction) reflects his study of evolutionary biology and his familiarity with the ideas of Darwin, of Wallace, and of contemporary scientists. His depiction of posthistoric mankind in terms absolutely consistent with established biological principles makes *The Time Machine* a quintessentially inventive work of anthropological fiction.

As a barometer of its age, and as an aspect of the broader cultural reaction to the work of science, imaginative writing may complement the history of science in any given period. Thus, if one wants to learn about human evolution from the viewpoint of the early 1900s, one can read academic textbooks of the period and supplement this reading with the fiction of Verne, of Burroughs, and of Rosny. As I have already suggested, and as I will demonstrate in greater detail, these works reflect not only intellectual commitments but personal struggles. It is not unique, for instance, that the endorsement of a scientific or medical idea can have grave spiritual consequences for a religious person who values the pursuit of scientific truth. The endorsement of creationism in the fiction of Verne and Burroughs, and Rosny's creative affirmation of the fossil record, all involved serious choices and commitments. The articulation of these choices and the transformation of normal into imaginative science will be the substance of this survey.

1

Heterogony and
H. G. Wells's
The Island of Doctor Moreau

Robert M. Philmus observes that, for Wells, "the idea that nature … has a *telos*, a purpose or intent in conformity with human ideals, was part and parcel of an anthropocentric view of nature that Darwin provided decisive evidence against" (*EW*.7). At every turn in the biological writings, Wells contests the idea of teleology, the doctrine that there are designs and causes in nature. This stance is what makes *The Island of Doctor Moreau* so ironic. On the one hand, Doctor Moreau's transformation of apes (and of other mammals) into quasi-humans flatly controverts Darwin's theory of evolution. Yet this un–Darwinian aspect of the story (which I identify as *heterogony*) will also subvert the scale of nature, a scheme purporting to explain the origins and interrelationships of all living things in aprioristic and static terms. In *The Island of Doctor Moreau*, Wells questions the validity of the Great Chain of Being and its configuration of the organic world "as a series of links or gradations ordered in a hierarchy of creatures, from the lowest and most insignificant to the highest," that is, to divinity (Formigari 325).

Redefining man's natural history in Darwinian rather than in classical or Judeo-Christian terms, Wells supplants the ladder concept with a more organic and realistic model. Scholars have recognized this strategy at work in Wells's fiction. Robert Philmus is certainly correct when he says that Wells thinks the essence of man and animal to have been "continuous" with each other ([1970]:120–1). Wells's purpose, in *The Island of Doctor Moreau*, according to John R. Reed, is to show that all life "is germane to all life," and that "Man himself is the only alienating power in the universe because he can *conceive* himself as separate from the *bios*" (146). Recently, Pascale Krumm has re-affirmed Wells's intention in the novel: to stress "that man and ape actually share a common ancestry as members of ... evolutionary side branches" (54). Although the transformation of the Beast-Folk is an instance of artificial rather than of natural selection, Wells nonetheless criticizes "false understanding of Darwin's theory" (Krumm 58).

Apparently, Wells had some knowledge of heterogony, the early species concept which is defined as "the conversion of one species into another one" (Mayr [1982]:872). Aristotle, Theophrastus, and Virgil promoted this idea, as did early botanists and herbalists (Mayr [1982]:254). It is present, for example, in the zoological mythology of Ovid's *Metamorphoses*, in which ants are transformed into men (Myrmidons VII. 635–43), and in which are found hybrids such as Minotaurs (bull-man; VIII.152–82) and Centaurs (horse-man; XII.216–36). The images of Zeus grappling with a man-horse giant or of the human struggle with giants and Centaurs, displayed in the art, architecture, and religion of ancient Greece, dramatize the Greek idea of humanity's heroic struggle against "the bestial element" (Grant 113–14). This myth recurs in Moreau's zoological transformations.

Although heterogony involves the transformation of one animal species into another, it should not be confused with *transformism*. The biological doctrine of transformism postulates that "existing species are the product of the gradual transformation of other forms of living beings," and that these changes are inheritable (*OED*). In the eighteenth century, transformism developed within a biological world-view governed by the Bible. Naturalists such as John Ray (in *Historia plantarum generalis* [1686–1704]) and Carl Linnaeus (1707–1778) (in *Fundamenta botanica* [1736]), subscribed to the idea that God had created all species on the fourth day of Creation, and that each was fixed and immutable (Rostand 510–26; Serafini 135–6). Although Linnaeus adhered to the Genesis story of Creation, he realized that he needed to account for observed variations within a given species (Rostand 514–15). In 1742, he acknowledged that sudden variations accounted for new genera arising in the plant kingdom, an acknowledgement contradicting the idea that species were immutable (Rostand 514–15). Speculations in this area were not restricted to botany. Georges Buffon (1707–1788), for instance, applied the theory of limited variability to the relationship between man and ape (Rostand 515–16; Serafini 154–6, 157–8).

The most important contributor to transformist doctrine, as far as

The Island of Doctor Moreau is concerned, was Pierre Louis Moreau de Maupertuis (1698–1759), a French mathematician and astronomer. In his *Essai sur la formation des corps organisés* (1754), he hypothesized that generation is the consequence of "seminal molecules" which, if normally combined, produced offspring resembling the parents; but if the molecular combination was abnormal, then unique and abnormal offspring resulted (Rostand 516–17). De Maupertuis' idea that species arose from the descent of abnormal characteristics identifies him as a direct antecedent of Hugo de Vries (1848–1935), the Dutch botanist whose work led to the discovery of spontaneously occurring mutations. Because de Maupertuis did not conceive of the gradual and continuous improvement of a species through the reproduction of the best-adapted individuals (that is, natural selection), his contribution to pre–Darwinian thought had its limits (Mayr [1982]:329). Nonetheless, Wells recognized the relevancy of de Maupertuis' work to his own. A number of common issues (family name, experimental interests, unconventional beliefs, life history, and common imagery) convince Ian F. Roberts that de Maupertuis is actually Doctor Moreau's "historical precursor" (272, 274). Roberts' research is a wonderful piece of detective work. We must also realize that de Maupertuis' idea of transformism is not equivalent to heterogony.

Both heterogony and transformism share the common principle that one species can change into another. The former expressed this transformation mythically, whereas the latter, as a forerunner of genetic theory, did so in terms of observed variations in living organisms. It appears, however, that what Moreau does to animals in his laboratory has more in common with heterogony than with transformism because he not only changes one species into another, but also surgically combines heterogeneous forms. Another reason for calling Moreau's work heterogonic is because of the biomedical ambiguity of his procedures. Moreau's explanation to Prendick regarding his earlier work on organ transplantation, oncology, and blood transfusion, disciplines essential to his current endeavors (*M.Var.*46–7), only partially dispels this ambiguity. Consequently, without background information on then-current biomedical research, we cannot fully appreciate the implications of Moreau's work.

Since heterogony is a mythological concept, it is surprising to discover it at all in Wells's work, especially since his position on evolutionary biology, expressed in his scientific discourse, is iconoclastic and firmly in the Darwinian camp. Robert Philmus correctly states that, to Wells, *Homo sapiens sapiens* is "an accident," and an "episode of natural history" (*EW*.8). Under the superlative shadow of Huxley, "the acutest observer [and] the ablest generalizer" (*Autobiography* 159), Wells defends

Darwin while derogating anthropocentric or "Excelsior" biology, and this sentiment reverberates throughout the early prose. In "Zoological Retrogression" (September 1891), for example, he rejects unilinear theories of evolution, especially those conferring on man a privileged and permanent place in natural history. Unlike the early transformists who worked within the limitations of the scale of nature, Wells apprehends natural processes in dynamic and temporal terms. Organisms (including man) avoid extinction and adapt through retrogressive solutions, for the evolution of species along divergent lines and from intermediate forms need not necessarily be an ascent. That man, like any other organism, is subject to extinction is the theme of the article "On Extinction" (September 30, 1893). The maturity of a species and the rapidity with which it may change through natural selection are the foci of "The Rate of Change in Species" (December 15, 1894); here, Wells suggests that *Homo sapiens sapiens*, as a species, is stagnant as far as non-acquired variation is concerned. In "The Biological Problem of To-Day" (December 29. 1894), he surveys the history of embryology and gives special emphasis to August Friedrich Leopold Weismann's (1834–1914) theory of the germ plasm, a theory supporting Darwin over Lamarck. Weismann (1834–1914), a German biologist and one of the founders of genetics, hypothesized that every living organism contains a hereditary substance ("germ plasm") (Serafini 206). In 1892, he averred that chance mutation alters genetic material. Weismann's theory superseded Lamarck's which held that acquired bodily changes can be inherited. Wells's essays "The Duration of Life" (February 23, 1895) and "Death" (March 23, 1895) reflect both on longevity and on natural selection. "Human Evolution, an Artificial Process" (October 1896), a significant essay, defines man in biological and social terms: the product of inherited factors and of natural selection, man is "obstinately unchangeable" and has ceased to evolve morphologically (*EW*.217). But man has continued to develop artificially, and this inveterate ability to adapt and to control changing environments is the consequence of human tradition, of suggestion, and of "reasoned thought" (*EW*.217). The early writings evidence Wells's conviction that the human species is subject to the laws of nature, that it holds no preconceived place in Creation, and that it is not immune to extinction.

How precisely does heterogony work in *The Island of Doctor Moreau*? Simply put, it efficiently replaces the vertical paradigm of Creation with a horizontal one in which man is a being *among*, rather than *above*, the animals (italics added). More than that, the idea of humanness is no longer the exclusive endowment of man. In fact, throughout the novella, either Wells reverses the characteristic behaviors of man and animal, or he simply does not distinguish between these two categories as they pertain to the sixty-seven creatures (including the three human beings) on the island (*M.Var.*57). Moreau's overarching purpose is to dispense with natural scales and taxonomic categories by subsuming all mammals on his island under the human species. As a result, a horizontal as opposed to a vertical phylogeny brings a new perspective to bear on human prehistory since it manifests a new relationship between man and the higher apes.

Since Prendick and Moreau are woefully imperceptive of the biological realities around them, the burden of interpretation is on the reader. Because Prendick's account of biological phenomena is dubious, I therefore disagree with Roslynn D. Haynes' notion of him as "a relatively objective" appraiser of island events whose opinions balance "the excesses of Moreau and Montgomery" (202). On the contrary, through no fault of his own, Prendick is ignorant of events anterior to his arrival, and his resulting imperceptiveness consequently obscures important biological information.

One example of Prendick's anthropological short-sightedness occurs when the ape-man of the main text scrutinizes his own hands (*M.Var.*35). Unlike Verne's explorers who, as we shall see, are acutely aware of the Waggdis' hands and feet, anatomical features speaking volumes about evolutionary heritage, Prendick is at a disadvantage inasmuch as he thinks these beings are injured natives. Excited to find that both he and Prendick share the anatomical trait of five fingers, the creature rejoices in this and counts Prendick's fingers out loud. Unfortunately, Prendick has no way of knowing what this gesture means in zoological terms. He wrongly thinks that the ape-man is merely demonstrating that his own hands are not malformed, like those belonging to less fortunate Beast-Folk. Consequently, Prendick interprets the ape-man's hand extension mundanely as a greeting.

The ape-man's gesture, to my mind, may have been intended to inform Prendick of their primatological kinship and common heritage, dramatically emphasized through Moreau's activities. More than asserting that *Pongo pygmaeus* and *Homo sapiens sapiens* are members of the primate order, the ape-man (likely an orangutan) reasonably implies that five fingers (and two opposable thumbs), along with the ability to speak, are traits certifying his membership in the family of *Homo sapiens sapiens* itself; additionally, the ape-man displays the brand of punishment, received from Moreau for ape-like jabbering (*M.Var.*39). The ape-man does not appear to vilify his torturer; rather, the initiatory scar is, for him, an emblem of his humanity. Believing that the ape-man is a degraded human being, Prendick questions him about how long he has been on the island, to which the ape-man responds by holding up three fingers cryptically. Since this response is also obscure, Prendick rashly concludes that he is an idiot. That the three fingers may refer not to the ape-man's natural age but to his post-operative existence on the island—that is, to his three or four months of self-consciousness—Prendick could never have guessed.

Whereas Verne's protagonists, Cort and Huber, would likely have thought Sturmius a missing link on the threshold of humanity, Prendick is unaware that the most cultured anthropoidal man on the island was actually once an ape. Once again, Prendick assumes he is a native who survived Moreau's butchery. In an ironic reversal of roles, Sturmius thinks Prendick is an ape whom Moreau humanized. The ironic truth is that both Sturmius and Prendick are animals who happen to be human beings as well: their taxonomic identities are intentionally blurred to assert man's animal origins and his zoological kinship to the apes.

Sturmius's humanity is dramatically illustrated in his conflict between civic duty and self-government, specifically with respect to whether he can repress his arboreal instincts. The interchange between these human beings is revealing and humorous. Sturmius is designated Prendick's mentor, by order of the Beast-Folk's court, when the latter is brought to trial for conversing with a hog-man on a number of illicit subjects, namely quadrupedalism and drinking from saucers. When Prendick is acquitted, he and Sturmius exchange views more candidly. Believing Prendick to be a humanized beast, Sturmius discourses on the prevalence of vice in his community but then asks Prendick if he ever had the irrepressible urge to run on all fours, to eat raw things, or to claw the bark of trees. The question troubles Prendick since he believes his interlocutor to have been a demented human victim of Moreau's science. Sturmius then reflects on the tensions in his community and on how the municipal infrastructure (vigilance committees, police, and magistracy) diligently suppress vice. Despite these measures, and although citizens go about their daylight business, walking erect and with modesty, nocturnally many "prowl ... on all fours," scenting their ways and howling (*M.Var.*123).

Apparently, if Sturmius's account is trustworthy, Moreau was unable to repress or eradicate the instinct of nocturnal predation. To a degree, Prendick's insight sharpens at this point. Astonished by the creature who, with "lank hairy arms & anthropoid visage," laments the demoralization of the island, Prendick contemplates the most fundamental question of the milieu—"was he an ape-man or a man-ape"? (*M.Var.*124)—a question preoccupying the great anthropologists of the times, especially in the light of DuBois' controversial discovery.

Even though Sturmius is a transmuted orangutan, the product of heterogony, he is a compassionate individual, standing midway between two species and overlooking the gulf between man and beast. Assuming that Prendick must undergo more agonizing procedures, he cautions him not to return to Moreau. Although Sturmius comprehends neither the nature of Moreau's work nor his own history, he dimly recalls the House of Pain (*M.Var.*124). Confiding this dim recollection to Prendick, he exhibits his orangutan heritage, precipitously swinging into the trees, and, in the process, violating a cardinal dictate of the Law (*M.Var.*124). But, in doing so, he asserts his natural identity as a humanized arboreal ape, dignifying himself in and against Moreau's artificial world.

Prendick remains ignorant of the fact that Sturmius is Moreau's crowning achievement: an anthropoidal man, both emotionally and morally his creator's superior. The missing link, in this case, is more genuinely human (and more humane) than his maker. The Moreauvian ethic, expediently designed to control the denizens of the island, self-destructively breeds rebellion because it forces the Beast-Folk to deny their genetically inalterable instincts.

Prendick does not appreciate primate language capabilities, finding the ape-man's incessant jabbering entertaining though hardly evocative. His ignorance is demonstrated by the way in which he scoffs at the ape-man's virtuosity with language. Although the ape-man speaks gibberish, he nonetheless coins new words (*M.Var.*89). This phenomenon which Prendick derogates as mimicry or idiocy actually demonstrates high intelligence. In the first place, Prendick appreciates neither Moreau's restructuring of the ape's vocal apparatus for speech nor the ape-man's ability to classify and then to differentiate headings and words. One category of words and thoughts is "Little Thinks," pertaining to the mundane interests of life (*M.Var.*81). A second, "Big Thinks," involves the learning of languages and the construction of neologisms. The creature memorizes and imitates Prendick's words (which is precisely how a child learns) and then repeats them to the milder or more receptive Beast-Folk. To Prendick, however, this is a nonsensical practice (*M.Var.*81). But there is every reason to believe that the ape-man, in exercising his language skills through the creation of new words, is trying to fashion a vocabulary to express abstract thought, for which the limited vocabulary at his disposal simply is inadequate.

Because Moreau is blind to the extent of his success, he, too, is an ironic figure whose opinions on his own work cannot be accepted at face value. In fact, the creator is oblivious to the wonder of his creation. For example, he cultivates the anthropoidal intellect yet derogates the extraordinary achievements of his creation. The history of an ape-man (likely to have been Sturmius), in a late 1894 revision of the text, illustrates this point. Moreau recounts to Prendick how he transformed an orangutan into his first "man" (*M.Var.*133), the orangutan, in this variant, becoming Moreau's keen-witted pupil who will learn rudimentary writing, reading, and math. The orangutan, beginning with a clean mental slate, recalls neither his simian past nor Moreau's procedures. Because of its mild and abject demeanor, the Kanakas educate him, and he builds his own house (*M.Var.*133). With his ability to read, the creature also acquires moral ideas (*M.Var.*133).

Wells re-worked the 1894 variant on Sturmius for the main text of 1896. There, Moreau educates a gorilla rather than an orangutan for three or four months (*M.Var.*49) (perhaps this is what the ape-man meant when he raised three fingers to Prendick). Moreau teaches the creature basic skills until it can speak. An adept craftsman (a builder of shanties), the gorilla-man reads at approximately the first-grade level, attains basic moral ideas but regresses into beastly "habits" (*M.Var.*50). When the creature climbs a tree to gibber at the Kanakas (*M.Var.*50), however, Moreau deems his experiments a failure. In the face of the momentary regression of the creature, Moreau, once again, seems not to have appreciated the extent of his achievement. The realization that he could neither document his findings adequately nor produce a living specimen for examination may have precipitated his retreat from professional circles; a conventional presentation, it is implied, would have been impossible without this evidence. Moreau's self-criticism is unrelenting: he is angry with himself for having made a man-like ape (not an ape-like man) and for the impermanence of his work. In the main text, this primate is clearly anthropoidal, lacking the "inward sinuous curve of the back which makes the human figure so graceful" (*M.Var.*50). Unable to laugh in the truly human sense, it only chatters or grins (1913 edition), a far cry from the eloquent Sturmius.

Moreau's inability to apprehend what defines humanity prevents him from understanding the genuine extent of his physiological success: that he has actually transformed apes into men even though these creatures would eventually revert to their original species. Narrowly focused on the physiology, he is oblivious to the profound evidence of humanity; for example, the ability to read, to write, to compute, to think abstractly, to devise technology, and to participate in ritual. To Moreau, all of this is inconsequential while physical retrogression is definitively significant. Thus, when the anthropoidal man is caught tree-climbing, Moreau is incensed. The physiological criteria for humanness are, in Moreau's mind, incontrovertible and do not allow for such actions. This narrow-mindedness, no doubt, reflects the scientific creator's insensitivity to suffering, human or otherwise, along with his misanthropy. Moreau's incapacity to recognize the humanity that he has fashioned ironically places his own lack of humanity into sharp relief.

Wells believes that in order to understand humanity one has to accept mankind's place in nature. To this end, he emphasizes that human beings and apes belong to the superfamily Hominoidea and, like Huxley in 1863, hopes to distinguish humanity in light of, rather than in opposition to, his animal origins and affinities. Wells criticizes the fixed-species concept of the scale of nature, as well as its anthropocentricity, through the transformation of men into animals and of animals into men. In this middle-ground, he carries Huxley's work on the comparative anatomy and embryology of primates to a misanthropic conclusion. While Huxley, in "On the Relations of Man to the Lower Animals" (1863), affirms that "Our reverence for the nobility of manhood will not be lessened by the knowledge, that Man is, in substance and in structure, one with the brutes" (by virtue of rational speech especially) (132), Wells implies that the nobility of man is a mercurial attribute.

In *The Island of Doctor Moreau*, Wells supplants the scale of nature with a mythological convention that underscores the phenomenal character of man. In using a pseudo-scientific convention (heterogony) to nullify the scale of nature, he counteracted a system that many believed unjustifiably exalted man's place in creation.

2

"A point in common": Pierre Boulle's *The Planet of the Apes*

Unlike Wells who employs pseudo-science ironically to make an assertion about scientific philosophy, Pierre Boulle, in *The Planet of the Apes* (1963), uses pseudo-science as the groundwork of a social allegory. To put Boulle's thinking into theoretical perspective, we need to have at our disposal a brief outline of the prehistory of the primate order which includes both ape and man.

Primate Prehistory

According to Eric Delson and Ian Tattersall, to whose survey of primate prehistory I am indebted here, both man and ape descended from an unknown common ancestor, 28 to 35 million years ago (481–84). From this main trunk, the hylobatid family (to which the modern gibbons belong) diverged 17 million years ago. A second divergence occurred between 13 and 16 million years ago when the orangutan lineage, whose prehistoric ancestors include *Sivapithecus* and *Ramapithecus* (once believed to have been hominid precursors), broke away from the main line of descent, leaving the common ancestor of the gorillas, of the chimpanzees, and of man as a solitary species; the subfamily Homininae is the zoological name for this ancestral species while the orangutan group is called the pongine. Many authorities believe that the gorilla line of descent separated into a distinct species between 6.0 and 10 million years ago, leaving the common ancestor of the chimpanzee and of man as the solitary representative of the Homininae. This evolutionary familiarity accounts for the close genetic kinship of the chimpanzee and man which is said to be 99.6 percent (Wrangham and Peterson 40).

Precisely when the chimpanzee became differentiated from the hominines, leaving the hominids as the sole representative of that group, is not known for certain although Wrangham and Peterson postulate the time as 5.0 million years ago (42). *Australopithecus afarensis* (rather than *africanus*) is thought to have been the likely forerunner, appearing between 2.5 and 3.0 million years before the present (an idea presently being modified). The *Australopithecine* species disappeared with the advent of *Homo habilis*, the first genuine member of the genus *Homo* (2.0 to 1.5 million years before the present), and *Homo erectus* (1.6 million to 300,000 years ago) succeeded *habilis*. More than two million years ago, a variety of hominids existed while modern man made his appearance 35,000 years before the present. During this archaic twilight (300,000 to 35,000 years ago), a period of which we know very little for certain, hominids possessed a variety of primitive and modern traits. It was an important moment for the future of mankind: during this period, *erectus* (many believe) gradually evolved into early-modern man.

In view of the immense time-spans involved in primate evolution, and since the common ancestor (the greatest ape of all) lived nearly 35 million years ago, a plot involving the interrelationship of these ancient creatures requires great care. For the sake of plausibility, one can consider several periods in this vast history to be worthy of imaginative exploration. Between 6.0 to 10.0 and 2.0 million years before the present, the ancestors of the chimpanzee and of man roamed the African savanna with at least the proto-gorilla as a co-inhabitant. At the same time, and for some unknown reason, the evolution of the hominids began. All hypotheses on the origin of the hominids focusing on the appearance of *afarensis* commence at the point when the chimpanzee divergence transpired: at ca. 4.0 million years ago, man separated from the hominine trunk, and the pioneer was *afarensis* (as most agree). This hominid, the forebear of the genus *Australopithecus*, lived from 4.0 to 3.0 million years ago and was followed by three or four variants (depending on whose theory you accept). According to one model, *afarensis* gave way to *africanus* (3.0 to 2.5 million years ago) whose existence overlapped with that of the short-lived *A. aethiopicus* (2.5 million years ago). *Australopithecus boisei* succeeded *A. aethiopicus* 2.75 to 1.8 million years before the present; and *A. robustus*, 1.5 to 2.0 million years ago, superseded the former. *Habilis*, the predecessor of erectus, appeared 2.0 million years ago; for a time, these two species of the genus *Homo* lived concurrently. As I parenthetically suggested, *afarensis*, known from the Lucy skeleton, may not have been a direct human ancestor after all. For paleontologists in Africa have recently unearthed a 3.5-million-year-old skull that points to an entirely new branch of human development (Wilford [2001]:A1, A10).

The paradigm I outline above is the evolutionary context of Boulle's story—that is, if he were conscious of the need for verisimilitude in the creation of a parallel primate history. Had Boulle been cognizant of the need for verisimilitude, then two fertile periods of inquiry would have manifested themselves: in one, the homininae are segregated from the hominids; in the other, modern humans are differentiated from archaic ones. At each of these transitional nodes—ca. 4.0 and 3.0 million years ago, respectively—our humanness, our character, and our collective past were determined. An imaginative endeavor at either node of human pre-history, however, demands a thorough familiarity with current paleoan-thropological and primatological information so as to maintain credibility. The alternative is that such a story risks degrading into either fantasy or absurdity. The word *fantasy*, in this context, denotes a supposition rest-ing on "no solid grounds," one that, if developed as planned, would be whimsical (*OED*). An *absurd*, unlike a fantastic, premise actually contra-dicts reason or truth (*OED*). The crucial differences between credible, fantastic, and absurd treatments of a primatological theme can be illus-trated this way. Generally, the premise that man or chimpanzee may be engineered for artificial insemination to succeed does not appear inher-ently absurd, given current scientific trends and capabilities, and the fact that the two species are 99.6 percent identical genetically. Even if it is impossible to perform such a procedure at the present time, it is likely that scientists and science-fiction writers can conceptualize its success while, at the same time, achieving some degree of credibility. The concept and its possible realization, in all likelihood, can provide the fictional writer with a starting point from which to move from a hypothetical into an imaginative realm. The difference between credible or inventive fiction, on the one hand, and fantasy, on the other, lies in the accurate use of up-to-date scientific information as the background of the story. I distinguish between authentic science and fantasy in this manner. If an author uses the idea of cross-species fertilization in the fiction but neglects to furnish a technically viable explanation of how this can be achieved, then the story is definitively fantastic, for it lacks a factual basis. The farther fiction moves away from authentic or normal sources, the closer it gets to absurdity. If, for example, the method of cross-fertilization is unbelievable or incom-pletely described, then the fiction is absurd, for it is contrary to truth and reality. One year before *The Planet of the Apes* appeared, Loren Eisley wrote these instructive words about how man and ape relate to one another genealogically: "He who sees his forebears in the great jaws and massive five-hundred pound body of a gorilla is seeing what has never existed, even though a half-human aura lingers pathetically around these mighty, unfortunate beasts who are doomed to early extinction" ("Epilogue" 248). Apparently, Boulle had not taken these facts into account.

Parallel Primatology

We can now relate the fictional text to its scientific background. Ulysses Mérou, Boulle's space traveler, discovers that the primatological reality obtaining on the parallel world of Soror is an inversion of primate history on Earth. Although, on Soror, ape and man are both bipedal, *Homo sapiens sapiens*, lacking rational thought and language, belies his majestic name (34–5). The chimpanzee anthropologist, Zira, informs Mérou that, one century earlier, Sororite naturalists had made "some remarkable progress in the science of origins" (94). Since Sororite anthropology parallels that of Earth, the prevailing opinion on creation (in their equivalent of the nineteenth century) was aprioristic and governed by theological premises that "species were immutable" and "created with their present characteristics by an all-powerful God" (94). Pioneering chimpanzee thinkers, the Darwin, Wallace, and Huxley of their day, radically modified these ideas. Thanks to their revolutionary thought, it is now known that "all species are mutable and have a common source" (94). Zira stipulates, however, that this does not mean that apes descended from man-like ancestors, which is an ironic inversion of an idea often misattributed to Darwin that man descended from ape. Instead, Zira offers a more accurate statement of the common ancestry of pongid and hominid: "Ape and men are two separate branches that have evolved from a point in common but in different directions, the former gradually developing to the stage of rational thought, the others stagnating in their animal state" (94). Zira is referring to a parallel event that transpired at some point between 28 and 35 million years before the present on Earth. The difference is that the hominid divergence, occurring at this ancient juncture, proved to be a dead-end whereas the apes (orangutans included) remained an undifferentiated order until, at some time, this family underwent a tripartite subdivision into separate but intellectually ascendant species. Zira even goes so far as to exhibit a taxonomic branch diagram. From its common ancestral point, she describes a divergent anthropoidal line with its dead-end offshoot representing man (95). This is the lineage of Anthropoidea (a term Boulle uses). In the taxonomic lexicon, however, Anthropoidea refers to an extant lineage of the primate order com-

posed of higher primates: platyrrhine monkeys of the New World, along
with the catarrhine monkeys, apes, prehistoric and modern humans of the
New World (Rosenberger [1988]:31).

In Zira's taxonomy, the central stem continued to develop after the
human line had individuated itself (much like the early branching off of
the gibbons). The evolution of the anthropoids in the story is an ascent,
not a descent, suggesting a model similar to that of the scale of nature.
As the central stem rose, it gave birth "to different species of prehistoric
ape with barbaric names" (95); these creatures were pre-rational and analogous to the human precursors mentioned above. The central stem eventually culminated in Simius sapiens, the wise or knowing ape.

The pinnacle of evolution on Soror, according to the radical evolutionists in the story, features three apices (no pun intended) occupied by
the chimpanzee, the gorilla, and the orangutan (95). The history of human
evolution that the fossil record has disclosed on Earth and that is described
above is here attributed to the Hominoidea superfamily, with the notable
exclusion of man. For hominization, Boulle substitutes simianization.
According to Sororite primatology, there is strong anatomical evidence
for this: the ape's brain, which has developed and become organized, is
markedly different from man's, which has scarcely "undergone any transformation" (96). Zira ascribes this evolutionary blossoming to the ape's
four-handedness: the opposability of four sets of thumbs and toes helped
them to brachiate and to perceive spatial depth, in turn, giving them great
dexterity; tool use, brain development, and civilization then followed.

The true revolutionary in this story is a conservative historian. Cornelius, Zira's spouse, believes that a human civilization antedated the
dominion of the apes and that the evolutionary scenario ascribing primacy
to apes is really a myth. Cornelius surmises that the apes somehow assimilated human civilization. Initially, there are three possibilities: (1) the
ascent of the higher apes paralleled the gradual decline of man; (2) the
transposition of dominant species occurred cataclysmically (155–6)—
although it is difficult to imagine how a cataclysm devastated man without
affecting the apes; and (3) the transposition originally occurred through
a social conflict, specifically an anthropoidal reaction to servitude as man's
experimental subjects. Cornelius is certain that a race of human beings
similar to those on Earth once populated Soror and, for unknown reasons,
"degenerated and reverted to an animal state" (161). This transposition
originally was not a biological process, caused by mutation, natural selection, or environmental factors. At this point, Cornelius interjects a theological element into the primatological history of Soror. Apes did not
succeed man accidentally. This result was "foreordained in the normal

course of evolution" (162). To a degree, Boulle's socio-biology resembles Wells's in *The Time Machine* where the leisured classes and the workers are irrevocably segregated from one another. Although Cornelius's hypothesis will overturn Zira's scale of nature, his teleological assumption promotes the unfounded idea that the apes were destined to inherit the Earth.

Boulle resolves the debate when a human female is induced to recount her suppressed racial memories, supposedly dating back more than two millennia: "Under electrical impulses her recollections go back to an extremely distant line of ancestors: atavistic memories reviving a past several thousand years old" (171). Apparently, several thousand years ago, Sororite apes were tamed and used as servants and laboratory subjects. They seem to have been moderately intelligent, for Boulle has anthropomorphized them to a level similar to that in *The Island of Doctor Moreau*. In the two-tiered world of Soror, the enslaved apes become articulate, revolt against their oppressors, and seize their captors for use in cancer experiments (173). This knowledge vindicates Cornelius' theory: the apes inherited human civilization.

What Boulle does here is to resuscitate heterogony, for the apes are transformed by authorial fiat. The idea that social stress can somehow trigger an evolutionary leap in three species and over several millennia is implausible. The speciation that occurs in *The Time Machine*, as we shall see, would take place at some undisclosed point 800 millennia before the narrative present (the fictional chronology before the Time Traveller's arrival in the future is not indicated). According to current theory, it took a minimum of 3,000 millennia for chimpanzees to diverge from the homininae subfamily into a distinct species; and it took 500,000 years for the genus *Homo* to emerge from the shadowy lineage of the *Australopithecines*. Since speciation takes more than several thousand years to occur, Boulle's fictional portrayal of primate history is not credible.

Had Boulle published *The Planet of the Apes* later that decade, one wonders if its primatological content would have been any different. In that period, an unprecedented explosion in primate research occurred, and it is interesting to relate Boulle's fiction to these events. Of course, since the novel appeared in 1963, Boulle may not have been acquainted with the ongoing fieldwork although references to it were undoubtedly present in the popular press. At least a half-dozen animal behavioralists were at work during this period. According to David Pilbeam, George Schaller published his influential study of social organization and behavior of the mountain gorilla in 1963 (34–5). Three primatological studies were also ongoing in Africa: V. and F. Reynolds were working on the social and behavioral patterns of the rain-forest chimpanzees in 1965; Jane Van Lawick-Goodall was observing woodland chimpanzees; and J. Hani and A. Suzuki, in 1967, were doing the same in the savanna woodlands. In addition, in 1969, Charles Oxnard, of Oxford University, was performing mathematical studies of primate anatomy, while R. A. and B. T. Gardner were teaching sign language to chimpanzees. Surprisingly, none of these experiments had any direct bearing on Boulle's writing.

Only in the broadest sense, in my judgment, can this novel be said to reflect a concern for the behavioral relationships between species in the superfamily Hominoidea. What Boulle says about the social organization, the anatomy, and the language of these species has no bearing on reality, for the victory of the apes over man, though ethically justified, has little to do with the dynamics of speciation. At issue in *The Planet of the Apes*, then, is the author's failure to recognize, and to exploit successfully, the evolutionary possibilities of two crucial homininae divergences: that of the gorilla from the human-chimpanzee lineage and that of the chimpanzee from the hominids.

3

Chains and Links:
Jules Verne's
The Village in the Treetops

Scholars have acknowledged that Jules Verne's prehistoric fiction is based on *bona fide* scientific sources. Kenneth Allott notes that, on the issue of evolution, Verne was conversant with the authoritative scientific opinions of Karl Vogt (1817–1895), of Geoffrey Saint-Hilaire (1772–1844), and of Armand de Quatrefages (1810–1892) (147). Herbert R. Lottman recognizes the influence of published accounts of famous expeditions on Verne's adventure novels (95). Arthur B. Evans and Ron Miller credit Verne for having grounded his "novel of science" on scientific opinion; in fact, his research, involving reference books, scientific journals, and newspapers, was extensive (3–4). Judging from the use of science in *The Village in the Treetops*, it appears that Verne had more than a superficial knowledge of current anthropology. A related question, which interests me here, concerns the way in which Verne uses scientific material in his narratives. Evans demonstrates, in an earlier context, that Verne's "Voyages Extraordinaire" are more appropriately characterized as "scientific" rather than as "science" fiction since they customarily feature unalloyed scientific passages used didactically.

The dialogues between Cort and Huber, the African explorers, demonstrate that Verne was conscious of the need for verisimilitude. In the final analysis, he rejects the idea that the missing link is a lineal precursor of modern man. Deferring to the establishment, his fictive anthropologists maintain that the absence of religion in Waggdian culture, which supersedes morphological evidence to the contrary, disqualifies these hominids from membership in the human family. This conclusion reflects Verne's belief that "evolution and Scripture were irreconcilable" (Lynch 82).

Background on the missing link

From the middle of the eighteenth century up to the time of Darwin (Lovejoy 236), the idea of a missing link, "a hypothetical animal assumed to be a ... [connection] between man and the anthropoid ape" (*OED*), conformed to the vertical scale: all created beings descended from God and the angels down through man and the animals. Since nature had been accommodated to a Judeo-Christian world-view, speculations on human prehistory necessarily began with the Creation story in the book of Genesis: for this reason, prehistoric man was referred to as an "antediluvian" being, that is, as one living before the biblical Deluge. Moreover, the arcane scale or ladder of nature dictated that a missing link would simply be "the halfway stage" between man and ape (Mayr [1963]:343–4).

The figure of the ramifying plant, tree, or bush, a more accurate and Darwinian way of describing organic evolution, gradually supplanted the ladder or chain model. Jean Baptiste Lamarck (1744–1829) and Baron Cuvier (1769–1832), among others, modified the vertical construct, revising its zoological implications. Widening the horizontal dimensions of the vertical model into a branching tree, Lamarck theorized that offspring inherited acquired characteristics and had the capacity to adapt to their environments. Of Lamarck's contributions to the understanding of human evolution, three in particular influenced Darwin: that species are changeable rather than fixed; that they arise from older species over long periods of time; and that man had undergone a gradual transformation to his present state from "pithecoid" or ape-like origins (Haeckel 76).

The image of a "richly branching phylogenetic tree," as Ernst Mayr describes it, redefined the search for the missing link. Rather than an exclusive individual, ancestor to both man and ape, the missing-link concept came to mean an entire series of extinct ancestors, occurring in the branches of human history ([1963]:343–4). In 1891, a candidate for the missing link, *Pithecanthropus erectus* (Greek for "upright ape-man"), was discovered. Despite its primitive features, this hominid, which was two million years old, supposedly could speak, use tools, and employ fire (Mayr [1982]:621). Previously, Ernst Haeckel, in *The History of Creation* (1876), had logically inferred the existence of just such an ancient being (Reader 40). His thinking inspired Eugène Dubois (1859–1941), a young Dutch physician and amateur paleontologist, to search for the missing link in Indonesia (Heizer 125). Dubois excavated a skullcap from the bank of the Solo River, at Trinil (central Java), in 1892; and, a few years later, he retrieved a modern-looking femur. The fossils proved to be over two million years old (Heizer 125). In August 1895, Dubois presented the skullcap, femur, and two teeth to The Third International Congress of Zoology, held in Leiden (Heizer 125). Despite cynics and legitimate skeptics, Dubois remained convinced that he had found a missing link, a contention he expressed in the 1896 lecture, "On Pithecanthropus Erectus: A Transitional Form between Man and the Apes." Although the specimens were incongruent with one another (a humanoid femur and anthropoidal skull and teeth), he insisted that they belonged to a single "intermediate form" (Dubois 131). Rudolf Virchow (1821–1902), the renowned German pathologist and anthropologist, demurred on the grounds that Dubois could not definitively prove that the remains belonged to one individual (Dubois 132). Others who conceded that the fossils belonged to one creature could not agree on whether it was an ape-man or a man-ape. But Haeckel eloquently defended Dubois' findings in a paper read on August 26, 1898, at the Fourth International Zoological Congress at Cambridge (Reader 47). According to him, "the petrified remains of Pithecanthropus" disproved the charge that the ape-man was an illusion (quoted in Shipman [2001]:309).

Before Dubois' discovery, comparative anatomists had been investigating the possibility of their close biological affinity in order to illuminate the common past of man and ape. In "On the Relations of Man to the Lower Animals" (1863), Thomas Henry Huxley speculates about human development in terms of "the gradual modification of a man-like ape," and he postulates that modern humanity is the product of the same "primitive stock as those apes" (125). In this context, Huxley is not speaking of the transformation of one species into another but of a gradual development over enormous breadths of geological time. Through comparative embryology and anatomy, he establishes man's biological kinship to the higher apes but not at the expense of man's uniqueness and primacy in the animal kingdom.

Instead of arguing for mankind's unilinear descent from the apes, Darwin in *The Descent of Man* posits that humanity is "co-descendant" with other animals of a "common progenitor" (629): "a hairy, tailed quadruped probably arboreal in its habits, and an inhabitant of the Old World"; thus, *Homo sapiens sapiens* ought to be classed zoologically among the Quadrumana (632). These primates, in turn, are likely to have derived from "an ancient marsupial animal," the ancestry of which can be traced further along on a ramifying sequence of forms to some "amphibian-like creature." In the "dim obscurity of the past" stirred a "fish-like animal"; and the earliest precursor of the vertebrates was hermaphroditic, had lungs, a heart, and a brain (634).

An avenue of inquiry other than the paleontological, some thought, could provide more immediate knowledge about the missing link. Because the fossil evidence was scarce and obscure, nineteenth-century naturalists imagined the characteristics of a missing link by comparing modern native peoples to the higher apes (Eisley 338). The colonial and racist mentality of the times was largely responsible for the tendency to view dark-skinned people as being less than human. Thus, racists degraded native peoples into lower forms, anthropomorphized the apes, and then contended that, midway between degraded natives and upgraded apes, one could approximate a missing link.

One aspect of the confusion was that not enough was known about the apes. A body of literature that T. H. Huxley surveys in "On the Natural History of the Man-Like Apes" (1863) (one of Dubois' favorite texts [Shipman (2001):55]), illuminates the manner in which the explorers of the sixteenth and seventeenth centuries tended to anthropomorphize the apes they encountered. Samuel Purchas, in 1613, published a soldier's fabulous account of a kind of great ape, twice the size of a man, hairy all over, but "otherwise altogether, like men and women in their whole bodily shape" (11). In 1625, Purchas devoted a chapter to the story of the monster, Pongo, "in all proportion like a man; but ... more like a giant in stature than a man; for he is very tall, and hath a man's face, hollow-eyed, with long haire upon his browes.... He differeth not from a man but in his legs; for they have no calfe" (12–13). These creatures, ludicrously portrayed as savage killers, pummeled elephants to death with their fists, ran in packs, and were so strong "that ten men cannot hold one of them" (13). Since little was known in the 1650s about "Asiatic man-like apes," descriptions of them were similarly exaggerated (17). The English anatomist, Tyson, wrote the first scientifically accurate and complete description of the higher apes entitled, *Orang-utan, sive Homo Sylvestris; or the Anatomy of a Pygmie compared with that of a Monkey, an Ape, and a Man* (1699) (17). Although what Tyson calls a "Pygmy," and illustrates as a well-proportioned, hairy little man, turned out to have been a chimpanzee (18), his detailed comparison between the anatomy of the so-called "Pygmy" and that of other apes and man impressed Huxley. Comparative anatomy, Huxley rightly thought, was the antidote to wild stories.

The French naturalist Georges Buffon (1707–1788), among others, portrayed the higher apes less as "man-like apes" than as distinct species closely related to man. Buffon's, however, was a mixed view. On the one hand, he differentiated pongids from hominids and rejected the notion that species had absolute boundaries (Himmelfarb 170). On the other hand, he mistakenly believed that savage man and the ape had to be viewed comparatively so as to learn about man's natural history (Eisley 42–3). To view dark-skinned human beings as the linkage between mankind and their anthropoid ancestors derived from a theory called, "evolutionary monogenism." According to this theory, each race was assigned a specific level on the evolutionary "ladder," and (according to an extreme form of monogenetic thought) certain races were thought of as "ape-like" (Wolpoff & Caspari 116–117). Thus, descriptions of natives, rendered in anthropoidal terms, attempted "to equate the … evolution of man with a graded existing scale of creatures running from the ape to man" (Eisley 278).

To compare an ape to man anatomically rather than analogically was a legitimate and revealing endeavor. In "On the Relations of Man to the Lower Animals," for example, Huxley compared the skeletons of man and ape with the intention of answering the questions: "is Man so different from any of these Apes that he must form an order by himself? Or does he differ less from them than they differ from one another, and hence must take his place in the same order with them?" (85–6). In the course of his analysis, he stresses that, to the trained eye, gorilloid structures cannot be taken for their human counterparts; nor can the reverse occur since each is unmistakably different from the other. He makes the important taxonomic distinction that, "The structural differences between Man and the Man-like apes certainly justify our regarding him as constituting a family apart from them; though, inasmuch as he differs less from them than they do from other families of the same order, there can be no justification for placing him in a distinct order" (124). The key classificatory headings are, of course, "family" and "order." Though man and the higher apes are members of the primate "order," man alone belongs to the *Homo sapiens* "family." While comparative analysis establishing the common heritage of man and ape, Huxley was under no illusion that the study of the great apes furnished direct insight into human ancestry. On this salient point, he departed from those advocating unilinear evolution.

Scalar zoology was not just a curious and benign relic of the history of ideas in the West. It would have invidious consequences for mankind, one of which, as I mentioned, was to stimulate the construction of artificial classifications of human beings. An especially notorious one, popular in Darwin's time, was of a primate continuum comprising the European man, the Hottentot, and the orangutan, respectively (Eisley 260–1). The zoological dissociation of the "Hottentot" from the European, along with his conjectured proximity to the ape (as an extant analogue to the missing link), exemplifies the moral turpitude and distortions of the vertical scale of zoology. The term "Hottentot," first of all, does not describe an African tribe at all (*OED*). An Anglicized variant of "Hodmandod" was actually a pejorative used by mid–seventeenth century Dutch settlers for the Khoikhoi or Khoisan tribe of Southwest Africa and the Northwest Cape region (*OED*). The term *Hottentot* is itself an onomatopoeic word: European explorers are said to have used the Khoikhoi salutation literally (to the Dutch settler, the phonetic syllables *Hod-man-dod*) as a derisive cognomen for the people themselves. Another possibility, Boonzaier et al. point out, is that the name "Hottentot" originated as early as 1616 when the English traveler Edward Terry thought the click language of the Cape people sounded like the clucking of hens or the gobbling of turkeys (1). When a Dane heard the greeting song of the Cape people, another story goes, he transformed the expression "hautitou" into "Hottentott" which eventually came to be used in Europe to represent the native people of the Cape of Good Hope (1). Obviously, the name had little to do with the real people, who incidentally called themselves "Khoikhoi," literally meaning "real people" (1). Khoikhoi culture suffered further indignity when "Hottentot" acquired the English connotation of inferior intellect or culture (*OED*).

The influence of myth and the ignorance of sixteenth- and of seventeenth-century European explorers of the Cape, such as Augustin de Beaulieu and John Jourdain, branded the Cape people miserable savages and cannibals, and this stereotype reverberated in second-hand accounts and in the art of the period (Boonzaier et al. 8–10).

By the middle of the twentieth century, the natural history of man according to the scalar model had fallen into disuse. As Stephen Jay Gould explains, man was no longer seen as "the foreordained product of a ladder that was reaching toward our exalted estate," but as "the surviving branch of a once luxuriant bush" ([1986]:62). The idea of a single missing link on a vertical scale gave way to the idea of missing *links* diffused throughout Paleolithic time. It is worth reiterating that human evolution began in Africa during the Pliocene and early Pleistocene Epochs. The first hominid species (likely *habilis*, the first stone-tool maker) existed between 2.0 and 1.6 million years ago in eastern and southern Africa (Tattersall & Delson 484). The earliest *erectus* fossils (Haeckel's *Pithecanthropus erectus*), dated 1.8 million years ago, were of a contemporary of *habilis*, had a larger brain than that creature, and was able to hunt and manufacture more sophisticated stone tools than its predecessor. In Eurasia, *erectus* eventually evolved, ca. 1.0 million years ago, into archaic *sapiens*; and this form, in turn, diversified into sublineages such as that of the Neanderthal. Anatomically modern humans, appearing in Africa ca. 120,000 years ago, diverged into geographic groups or races throughout the world; and 30,000 years ago, modern humans completely displaced archaic forms.

Pithecanthropus erectus

By 1901, despite the Neanderthal, Javan, and Mauer discoveries, little was known about the late Pleistocene ancestors of man (Reader 57). *The Village in the Treetops* is therefore an interesting period piece and experiment in imaginative anthropology: it envisions the search for *Pithecanthropus erectus* not in the forests of Indonesia but in the jungles of Africa. Explorers in search of a lost primatologist, an expert on ape-language capability (a German named Johausen who had been following in the steps of an American, R. L. Garner), stumble upon a community of beings that appear to be incarnations of Dubois' *Pithecanthropus*. Verne tries to present his creatures, called the Waggdis, in believable terms; therefore, their anatomy is in keeping with Dubois' findings (or with reconstructions from these findings) and commensurate with Sir Arthur Keith's (1866–1955) opinion that Dubois' hominid was essentially human but of a lowly kind (Reader 56).

Verne's explorers, Cort and Huber, with the assistance of the narrator, make a number of salient observations about the unusual creatures they encounter in the jungle. No doubt, as Peter Costello has pointed out, Verne had viewed the sculpture of *Pithecanthropus* at the Paris Exhibition of 1900 (199). Dubois had made a life-size sculpture of the creature which he abbreviated as P.e., using as a model his son, Jean (Shipman [2001]:320–1). P.e. undoubtedly influenced Verne, and his explorers sound as if they, too, had visited the exhibition.

Verne rightly emphasizes anatomical characteristics. The Waggdis, report Cort and Huber, are "two-handed" rather than "four-handed" which means that they have opposable thumbs, not big toes, with which to grasp (155); moreover, they walk wholly upright and not on their knuckles. These anatomical features are very revealing. The divergent big toes of apes, Verne understood, are capable of grasping whereas human toes are short, with the big toe parallel to the others. These details, he realized, were vitally important inasmuch as the morphology of the four human toes transmits weight more adequately through the big toe which, in turn, provides the balance necessary to bipedalism (Pilbeam 62). In addition, the Waggdis have prominent human features: they lack a pre-hensile tail (which monkeys have); they have ear lobes (which apes and monkeys lack); and their "eyebrows do not beetle as do those of most of the simian race" (155). Although their noses are flattened (an anthro-poidal feature), the foreheads do not recede, and the skulls are round, all of which are features held in common with modern man. Although the facial anatomy presents a mixture of traits, the explorers justifiably con-clude that the Waggdis "took more after men than after monkeys in gen-eral appearance" (127–8).

To humanize the Waggdis (at least to a degree), and to recapitulate Dubois' findings with respect to P.e., Verne included a reference to their *facial angle,* to which he assigned a reading of 45 degrees. Petrus Camper of Leiden (1722–1789), the founder of craniometry (the science of mea-suring skulls), had proposed that the extent to which a jaw protruded was a direct index of a creature's primitivity and of its place in the vertical scheme of Creation. To determine this measurement, one could triangu-late lines from vertices on the lower part of the nose, on the cheekbone, and below the orifice of the ear (Camper 198). The more prognathic the face (and the more acute the angle), he thought, the more primitive the skull. The human facial angle, he estimated, ranged from 70 to 100 degrees.

For some inexplicable reason, Verne assigned an index of 45 degrees to the Waggdi which meant that they had snouts. His ostensible purpose was to emulate Dubois' specimen as it was embodied in the P.e. statue; but to do so required that the Waggdis have an angle in the 70 to 100 degree range, consistent with other cranial features, namely a brachy-cephalic or rounded skull and an unrecessive forehead. It seems, there-fore, that Verne made an error, for the description of the Waggdian skull, with the exception of the angle, does, in fact, correspond to that of a modern human: "Its head was rounded, its facial angle about forty-five degrees, its nose flattened, its forehead not receding" (128). A creature with a 45 degree facial angle could not have a flat nose, a round skull, or a vertical forehead.

Verne's concomitant purpose was to portray the Waggdis as inter-mediate forms. To this end, he had to make the skull anatomy less than fully human. Thus, John Cort points out that the Waggdian heads, though "rounded," possess an "almost human facial angle" and, though *slightly* prognathic, are "microcephalic" (italics added; 155). To a craniometrist, the small Waggdian skull, despite its modern external features, meant that this hominid had a level of intelligence below that of modern European man. This would have an important bearing on Verne's anthropology. His reference to microcephaly, along with the facial angle, means that he subscribed to contemporary pseudo-anthropology and to its assumptions about racial degeneration and superiority. Although Camper was not a racist, and although he was one of the first anatomists to distinguish man systematically from apes, his angular method was later used as the basis for racist theory and for polygenist scientific studies (Wolpoff & Caspari 64). One scientist who used Camper's anthropometric measurements to propagate racist assumptions was Baron von Cuvier (1769–1832), the French naturalist. In 1805 and in 1812, he reported that white Europeans, whom he thought to have been the most advanced of the races, had both larger facial angles and more fully developed foreheads than other races and groups (Finger 317–18). Since Africans were believed to be more prognathic than whites, Cuvier and others implied that they were less than human.

Microcephaly was also used as an index to evolutionary development, and it, too, had an invidious effect on how human beings were perceived. Those who attempted to fill the niche between man and ape on the vertical scale, as I pointed out, looked for living intermediates. One architect of this plan was the Genevan anthropologist Karl Vogt. In his *Antiquity of Man* (1864), Vogt imagined that microcephalic idiots were throwbacks to obsolete hominids (Eisley 266–70). This odious assumption states that a person deficient from birth in ordinary mental powers and whose cranium does not develop normally is not a human being. He reasoned that primate brain volume (as opposed to the cephalic index, a ratio between body and brain size) was a valid indication of evolutionary status. Thus, the microcephalic idiot represented an intermediate, evolutionary form, "which at a remote period may have been normal." "This arrest [as Vogt calls it] is the simian stage" (cited by Eisley 268). To demonstrate these assumptions graphically, advocates of vertical evolution placed the skulls of the modern African, of the microcephalic idiot, and of the chimpanzee on a continuum progressing to the modern, white European male (Eisley 268). Verne subscribed to the idea that the Waggdis, descendants of *erectus*, occupied a position in the graduated zone between the highest apes and (what the racist anthropology of the times considered to be) the lowest of men; hence, they were mentally deficient and quasi-human.

Although Verne had tacit doubts about the validity of the scale of nature and about theories fashioned in its image, he would not grant *erectus* full membership in the genus *Homo*. His intellectual and ethical ambivalence is illustrated in the text. On the one hand, although the third-person narrator rejects unilinear thinking, cautioning that "it must not be inferred that man is a perfected ape or the ape a degenerate man" (156), the humanity of the Waggdis ultimately depends on whether they possess "moral and religious characters peculiar to man," along with "the faculty of conceiving abstraction and generalizations," and "an aptitude for the arts, science, and letters" (157). If the Waggdis demonstrate these capabilities, then they are members of the genus *Homo*. The conundrum Verne faced, however, was irresolvable: to admit the Waggdis (and erectus) into the human family meant that human creatures pre-dated the story of human Creation in the book of Genesis. Their anterior existence could only be explained if they were judged to be either non-human or collateral dead-ends.

According to several criteria, one can argue that Verne's hominids are indisputably human: they control fire (148); their dentition is identical with that of man (156); and they are manufacturers (165). These criteria notwithstanding, Huber asks Cort a rhetorical question: "why not admit them into the ranks of humanity?" (166). At this crucial point, Verne defers to the religious establishment. Because the Waggdis have no concept of a supreme being which is reputedly common to most savage tribes (166) (a view Darwin rejected), they are definitively not human beings. Descendants of apes, they are in the aggregate a type "midway between the most perfect of the anthropoids and man" (169). The phylogeny of their species remains undefined but open to inquiry as they possess instincts uniting them with the animal kingdom—even though they have a "tincture of reasoning power" moving them towards the human race (169). So the intrigue surrounding Verne's Waggdis evaporates as these creatures are made to occupy a conventional taxonomic niche.

I. O. Evans is correct to say that the novel makes "a somewhat inconclusive suggestion" of the manner in which the missing link problem and the entire Darwinian controversy "might be solved" (Intro.9). Apparently, Verne was content with delineating the problem, with questioning the unilinear interpretation of primate evolution peripherally, and with evicting the Waggdis from the human family, based on their lack of religion. Overall, I think it fair to say that Verne proceeded with intellectual rigor even though he lost his nerve. Aside from the facial-angle mistake, his hominids closely resemble Dubois' reconstruction, the most cogent feature of which is its bipedalism. In this passage, Verne even mentions Dubois: "Their posture, similar to that of man, showed that they were in the habit of walking upright. They had a right to the term erectus given by Doctor Eugène Dubois to the pithecanthropus found in the forests of Java" (147). Yet Huber remains unsure of the Waggdis' nomenclature: "there is still lacking a rung in that ladder, a creature midway between the anthropoids and man, with a little less instinct and a little more intelligence" (104–5).

Between the early 1890s when Dubois made his discovery and 1901 when *The Village in the Treetops* was published, the missing link sensation abated considerably. Not surprisingly, it was an intellectually vacuous period for Dubois who wrote nothing on Trinil. Against this background, the value of Verne's fiction appreciates considerably since it might well have served to remind the reading public that their understanding of human evolutionary history had reached a turning point and involved serious unresolved issues. Ironically, his use of this subject matter was courageous. His retreat from controversy notwithstanding, we should recognize that even though he fictionalized the idea of the missing link and aired the most prominent theories, he risked charges of atheism. As Pat Shipman has recently pointed out, as late as the first decade of the twentieth century, human evolution "was still a dangerously controversial subject" ([2000]:334). One reasonable inference to be made is that, by fictionalizing the missing link story in the context of contemporary scientific research, Verne was encouraging readers to take a critical look at the subject of human evolution. Even though the author did not openly endorse the work of Doctor Dubois, his intriguing rendition of its content demonstrates his interest in the subject, judiciously avoids censure, and may have rekindled public interest in the subject, despite the oppressive atmosphere within which he wrote.

As a resource for knowledge about early twentieth-century paleoanthropology, *The Village in the Treetops* has unexpected value. It has since been determined that, for several hundred thousand years, populations of *erecti* originated in Africa and migrated to Asia later (Rightmire 259); Verne anticipated this fact. Second, he had some genuine insight into *erectus* culture, even though Waggdian ritual, sociology, and technology would not correspond directly to the rudimentary evidence found at future sites. I would like to outline briefly the fossil record of *erectus* from the early 1920s to the present and retrospectively compare this material with Dubois' conjectures and then with Verne's fiction.

As Philip Rightmire has explained, in the early 1920s, the anatomist Franz Weidenreich (1873–1948) found a trove of specimens in a cave in Zoukoudian, near Beijing, China. Although most of his specimens were lost during World War II, new fossils turned up afterwards (260). These included stone tools, animal bones, and evidence of fire. Since 1938, Indonesian sites have yielded additional relics. A Dutch paleontologist, Gustav H. Ralph von Koenigswald (1902–1982), made important discoveries in the Sangiran region of Java where more than forty human individuals have been found (Rightmire 260). The Southeast Asian sites have suggested that *erectus* fashioned tools. Since 1954, workers have been accumulating *erectus* specimens at Tighenif, Algeria, on the Atlantic coast of Morocco, at Salé, northwestern Africa, at Olduvai Gorge (Tanzania), in the Turkana basin in northern Kenya, and elsewhere (Rightmire 260–1).

These finds would clarify Dubois' conjectures about the anatomy of *erectus*. The femur (the only intact bone) that Dubois found and thought anthropoidal was clearly shaped for upright walking (Shipman [2001]: 208). An abundance of cranial bones have since come to depict *erectus* in a new light. Although the brain was, in fact, smaller than that of modern humans, it did have prominent browridges after all. The forehead is flattened (as per Verne's Waggdis), but there are strongly developed bony crests on the face that support heavy chewing muscles, and the chin is recessive, all of which are primitive traits. The skull morphology is, in this and in other respects, distinct from that defining the human skull. Yet one school of thought believes that *erectus* was modern man's direct ancestor, and that its emergence into modernity occurred perhaps less than 100,000 years ago. The controlled use of fire has been attributed to *erectus*, especially in mid–Pleistocene sites in Africa, Asia, and Europe although the evidence remains equivocal (Toth & Schick 208).

Verne's attributions of sophisticated stone-axe technology, of tree-top villages, of canoes, and of other basic manufacturing to the Waggdis, however, are wholly unfounded and do not correspond to what is known of middle Pleistocene Paleolithic sites (Toth & Schick 431). Hand axes have been found at *erectus* digs at Olduvai Gorge, at Zoukoudian (China), and at other locales, but the specimens are sparse. Fossils at Swartkrans, Olduvai, and Tighenif suggest that *erectus* did indeed make hand axes and similar stone tools in what has been called the Acheulian industry, the assemblages of which date from 1,500,000 to 200,000 years ago. It appears that the culture of *Pithecanthropus* (which Verne reputedly emulated) has more in common with *Homo sapiens sapiens* who lived ca. 40,000 to 10,000 years ago than with earlier hominids (Toth & Schick 433–4).

4

Phylosynthesis in Edgar Rice Burroughs' *The Land That Time Forgot*

In his tripartite saga *The Land That Time Forgot* (1924), Edgar Rice Burroughs (1875–1950) incorporates a disconnected array of hominid fossils into a systematic framework. In the process, he imagines a unique biological phenomenon, *phylosynthesis,* a term I have constructed from *phylum* (as in *phylogeny:* the "origin and evolution of a group or race of animals or plants" [*OED*]) and from *synthesis* ("the combining of parts or elements so as to form a whole, a compound" [*OED*]). Precisely what Burroughs attempts to do in his fiction is to unify the human phylum, conceptually, and to account for its origin and evolution.

Since paleoanthropological knowledge about early man in the 1920s was discontinuous, contradictory, and fragmentary, there was a need for a unifying theory to describe how ancient humans related, taxonomically, to one another and to modern human beings. To meet this need, Burroughs practiced his own kind of *systematics,* that is, the study of "the diversity of life and of the relationships among taxa, living and fossil, at the various levels of the taxonomic hierarchy (Tattersall [1988]:558).

Relative to his scientific milieu in 1924, however, Burroughs' innovative purpose appears to have had much in common with pre-Darwinian biological thinking in that it endorsed the scalar idea of natural development. His hominids, though classified, described, and related to one another, exist in a compressed temporal framework. As a result, human evolution is confined to, and replicated in, the natural history of each individual indigenous to Caprona, Burroughs' prehistoric world.

Unilinear biology and the scale of nature, it will become clear, govern the imaginative world of *The Land That Time Forgot*, despite the author's utilization of contemporary thought.

Scattered Intelligence

If we review the fossil inventory from the mid–nineteenth century to the end of World War I, we will find that neither the systematic pursuit of archaeological material nor its rigorous appraisal was the customary practice. Instead, discovery was haphazard and fieldwork chanceful. With the exception perhaps of Eugène Dubois, who was inspired more by Ernst Haeckel's logical inferences about the missing link than by a fortuitously unearthed bone, from 1848 to 1908, most workers benefited from good luck; however, since many of them were non-scientists, they often accidentally destroyed or damaged fossils during extrication. Even when professionals were able to retrieve accidental finds, their peer-reviewed presentations, beset by the lack of scientific method and of technical skills, elicited suspicion and scorn since radical ideas about human antiquity threatened the status quo. Even the most compelling evidence could be contested into oblivion and then consigned to archives.

J. B. de Perthes' (1788–1868) archaeological experiences constitute a case in point. A French customs official stationed at Amiens, de Perthes, in 1837, began to search for fossils haphazardly in gravel beds near Abbeville, France (Heizer 82–3). He found flint objects that seemed unusual. Despite his lack of training, he was able to discern that these bits and pieces were made of a different kind of stone than what was locally present, and some exhibited human workmanship (Heizer 82–3). While collecting this material, de Perthes made a case for human antiquity. Despite his eloquence and the impressiveness of his work, French learned societies ignored his efforts for many years (Campbell 59).

But de Perthes' persistence eventually paid off. Despite years of derision, he published his findings in the five-volume *De la Création: essai sur l'origine et la progression des êtres* (1838–41) and in *Antiquités celtiques et antédiluviennes* (three volumes, 1847–65) (Heizer 82–3). His observations were vindicated in 1859 and reprised in his *De l'homme antédiluvien et ses oeuvres* (1860). But it took twenty years for de Perthes' contribution to paleolithic archaeology to be recognized (Heizer 83) and only then because he had an abundance of material, the single-mindedness to pursue his cause, and the ability to communicate his work.

In 1860, de Perthes worked within the prescribed limits of the scientific and theological communities. The story of Noah was the geological referent for archaeologists of those times. Although the adjectives *antediluvial* and *diluvial* (the latter refers either to the Deluge *or* to glacial deposits) recur in his writings, conventional ideas on Creation would not dampen his enthusiasm. He recalls, in *De l'homme antédiluvien*, for example, how difficult it had been to make sense of the scattered material in the Abbevillian gravel pits. Nonetheless, he perceived a dynamic order in nature that he expressed figuratively: "this confusion of all eras," he ruminates, passed like "a caravansary of the passed generations, as though to characterize the periods" (de Perthes 85). This superficial disorder contrasts with the explicit information offered by "the diluvial formations" (i.e., glacial deposits), the rich, cross-sectional strata, in which "each period is clearly divided." De Perthes expressed his appreciation for the geological magnificence of the Menchecourt stratification. Nineteen meters thick and subdivided into sixteen layers, the stratification was an encrypted book which he confidently asserted would yield its geological secrets: "From induction to induction, one can thus learn, if not the age of the layers where our axes were found, at least the epoch when the diluvial formation was finished and could have served as the base of the peat formation" (93). He was reasonably certain that the "horizontally superimposed layers ... show us in capital letters the history of the past: the great convulsions of nature seem to be delineated there by the finger of God" (85).

In view of how immethodical the fieldwork tended to be during the mid-nineteenth century, it is amazing that de Perthes managed to gain recognition at all. Rejected by many of his peers (with notable exceptions), he turned to quarry workers for help in order "to mold them as skillful as myself" (de Perthes 88). With their help, he secured twenty flints which he submitted for professional examination. But despite the hard work, many of his colleagues, doubting his "good sense" (88), expressed misgivings about his undertakings.

De Perthes' uphill climb against both natural and cultural conditions was heroic. It is surprising to learn that accidental events, more than anything else, contributed to his discoveries. Circumstances favored him, as he recounts in *De l'homme antédiluvien*, for the area in which he worked would not have been accessible had it not been for "immense works undertaken for the fortification at Abbeville, the digging of a canal, the railroad tracks that were being built," all of these projects, from 1830 to 1840, revealing "numerous strata of diluvium" (*diluvium* here referring to glacial deposits) (87). The chalk comprising its base "rose 33 meters above the sea level," forming what he calls "an immense bench which, from the basin of the Somme goes to rejoin that of Paris, and thus advances towards the center of France" (87). Thanks to these great excavations, "a vast field" had been opened to his studies (87).

A half-dozen landmark events, from 1848 to 1908, illustrate the fortuitousness of paleoanthropological discovery. At Forbes' Quarry, on the Rock of Gibraltar, the skull of what was thought to have been a female Neanderthal, in 1848, was accidentally dislodged through blasting (Hrdlička 52). The most famous of all specimens, that of the Neander Valley, near Dusseldorf (Germany), was found accidentally at the Feldhofer Cave in 1856 (Campbell 63–4). Purely by chance did railway workers, in 1868, unearth four human skeletons while they were excavating under a limestone cliff. The site, called the Gorge d'Enfer, near the village of Les Eyzies (Dordogne region of southwestern France), produced four 35,000-year-old individuals who were anatomically equivalent to modern man, and who were called "Cro-Magnon," after the people who lived in the region (Campbell 66). In 1886, while digging in a cave near Spy, Belgium, two Neanderthal skeletons were accidentally found, along with the remains of extinct animals and chipped stone implements (Stringer [1988]:540); astonishingly, it took more than fifty years for these remains to be understood as belonging to archaic human beings (Campbell 65). As Pat Shipman recounts, in August of 1892, at Trinil, while Dubois was incapacitated with malaria, a native worker by chance hit the femur of the "missing link" with his shovel (Shipman [2001]:160). And the Mauer jaw (1907) was determined to have belonged to an *erectus*, a European relative of Dubois' missing link and, to date, the oldest European hominid. Once again, laborers unintentionally exhumed an invaluable piece of human history, damaging it in the process. Arles Hrdlička recounts the details:

> On the date of the find, two of the laborers were working in undisturbed material at the base of the exposure ... when one of them suddenly brought out on his shovel part of a massive lower jaw which the implement had struck and cut in two. As the men knew it was worth while to carefully preserve all fossils, the specimens were handled with some care. The missing half was dug out, but the crowns of four of the teeth broken by the shovel were not recovered. The men were struck at once with the remarkable resemblance of the bone to a human lower jaw; but it looked to him too thick and large to be that of a man [50–1].

The destruction of the jaw and the loss of the four crowns dramatize how priceless fossils could be crudely unearthed, and the process contrasts with the familiar image of fossil hunters abrading bone with dental instruments and brushes. In the case of the teeth, this clumsy act was especially tragic. To a comparative anatomist, teeth provide information about evolutionary relationships: workers are able to reconstruct phylogenetic and adaptive patterns of extinct animals, including those of human precursors, from dental remains (Kay 572, 571–8). With the loss of molar crowns went insights into what a hominid ate and how it lived. Moreover, the blundering exhumation of this *erectus* found no specialist on site. Determining its importance, then, was initially left up to the laborers and to the landowner.

Of particular importance to Burroughs' fiction would be the discovery, in 1908, of the La Chapelle-aux-Saints Neanderthal. About 60,000 years old, the cave site, in the Dordogne Valley, yielded the almost perfect skeleton of an old man (Stringer [1996]:301). Other remains were found in the area: at a cave near Le Moustier, at a rock shelter at La Ferrassie, and at one near La Quina (Stringer [1996]:297–98). All of this mind-boggling material, however, was misinterpreted. Pierre Marcellin Boule (1861–1942), a French paleoanthropologist and geologist, is well-known for his comprehensive though erroneous reconstruction of the European Neanderthal from the La Chapelle-aux-Saints skeleton (Spencer 97). Boule's monographs, published from 1911 to 1913, rejected the hypothesis that Neanderthals were the direct ancestors of modern man. Bernard Campbell delineated Boule's errors: his misconstruction of the bones made the Neanderthal appear ape-like; the misalignment of the foot bones, endowing this hominid with big-toe opposability, reinforced the simian depiction; because the knee joint was misinterpreted, it walked with a bent non-human gait; the spine was presumed, incorrectly, to lack the curvature needed for upright posture; the head was thrust forward unnaturally, to appear ape-like; the long, low skull was interpreted as signifying deficient intelligence (despite the large brain cavity). As a result, Boule concluded that this skeleton belonged to a disparate, extinct species, one unrelated to the genus *Homo* and certainly not a precursor of modern man (298–9). Coming from such an authority, this composite picture seemed definitive. For decades, research in this area slowed significantly.

I mentioned earlier in this chapter that Burroughs was unconcerned with the fossil record and with accurate dating. His fiction reflects this lack of concern since hominids temporally distanced from one another are portrayed as contemporaries in his story. The discoveries of the period from 1848 to 1908, however, tell us a quite different story. Of the three hominids discovered—*erectus*, Neanderthal, and Cro-Magnon—the first had the widest global distribution and the longest span of existence, ca. 2.0 million to 200,000 years ago. Western Asian and European Neanderthals lived between 70,000 and 50,000 years ago whereas all forms of Neanderthal lived from ca. 100,000 to 35,000 years ago. Modern humans, of whom Cro-Magnon man is representative, lived from ca. 90,000 to 24,000 years ago (Stringer [1988]:274). What these time-lines also tell us is that *erectus* disappeared as a discrete taxon 100,000 years before the advent of the first Neanderthals; therefore, if the fossil record we have is to be trusted, then Neanderthals and modern humans co-existed for 35,000 years. It would be hasty to conclude, however, that initially the *erecti* and then the Neanderthals became absolutely extinct at the 200,000 and the 35,000 year junctures, respectively. How the three related to one another remains a difficult problem. But the growing consensus about the middle to late Pleistocene history of man (the middle period extends nearly 127,000 years before the present) is that *erectus* would gradually evolve into modern man. According to Philip Rightmire, some posit that middle Pleistocene populations of *erectus* evolved "toward the anatomy characteristic of Homo sapiens," and they, including *habilis* (the precursor of *erectus*), "are linked in an unbroken progression of slowly changing forms" (259).

The idea of the close relationship of Paleolithic subspecies and of their co-existence at certain points on a continuum are inventive adumbrations on the part of Rosny in 1909 (as we shall see in chapter 9) and of Burroughs in 1924. Burroughs' model, however, appears quite fanciful when contrasted with later thinking. For example, diagrams purporting to represent human evolution in the Pleistocene—for instance, those of Philip V. Tobias (1967), of Louis Leakey (1971), and of John Napier (1971) (Campbell 132–3)—agree on only one line of continuity: that between habilis and modern man. The *erecti* and the Neanderthals, along with the *Australopithecines*, are either on the main-line or are side-tracked into extinction. Burroughs' pursuit of continuity had no basis in fact. For modern paleoanthropologists, the continuing lack of consensus on these relationships mirrors the paucity of natural evidence. This fact notwithstanding, the time-lines, based on recovered evidence, are rough indicators of longevity.

Phylosynthesis

I would like to consider three illustrations of Burroughs' fictional use of contemporary science. When Bowen J. Tyler, Jr., and his party arrive on the island of Caprona, the lost continent named after the early eighteenth-century Italian navigator Caproni (425), they find a corpse, the phylogeny of which is unclear: "it resembled an ape no more than it did a man" (59). The scale of nature, along with the idea that a missing link is one level below dark-skinned human beings and one level above apes, evidently shapes Tyler's paleoanthropological thinking. The creature they find has large toes that "protruded laterally as do those of the semiarboreal peoples of Borneo, the Philippines and other remote regions where low types still persist" (59). The "low types" to which Tyler refers are indigenous people who have been ascribed traits akin to orangutans, for protruding toes are characteristic of the great apes. In attributing this feature to indigenous Asians, Tyler is divesting them of their humanity. The creature's face is a composite, possibly "a cross between Pithecanthropus, the Java ape-man, and a daughter of the Piltdown race of prehistoric Sussex" (59). In crossing *erectus* with Piltdown, incidentally, one would have found no observable difference in skull size since Piltdown's was actually a human skull, and since erectus had a brain about 87 percent the size of modern man's (Rightmire 264). The *erectus* jaw, though noticeably different from that of modern man, to the trained eye, was not simian while the Piltdown mandible was indeed just that, for it had been planted at the site (as I will explain in detail in chapter 5). Tyler's observations in this regard are reasonably sound. What Burroughs is envisioning is an incarnate blend of P.e. and Piltdown, a being whose phylogenetic identity occupies a position between the human and simian levels on the Great Chain of Being.

A second example of Burroughs' reliance on contemporary theory occurs when Tyler's party encounters living hominids. One hominid resembles "the so-called Neanderthal man of La Chapelle-aux-Saints" (89). The description is worth reproducing, for its source is unmistakable:

> There was the same short, stocky trunk upon which rested an enormous head habitually bent forward into the same curvature as the back, the arms shorter than the legs, and the lower leg considerably shorter than that of modern man, the knees bent forward and never straightened [89].

The forward-bending head, the arching spine, the short, lower legs, and the unbent knees are all drawn from Boule's misconstruction of the Neanderthal specimen of La Chapelle. These anatomical characteristics, as noted above, propagated the image of the Neanderthal as a slouching, semi-bipedal imbecile. Burroughs' fiction is an unwitting purveyor of Boule's ineptitude and of cultural resistance to the idea of man's descent from archaic forms.

In a later encounter with living hominids, Burroughs demonstrates beyond a doubt that, for him, evolution is a progressive ladder. Tyler observes a group of creatures who are "human and yet not human" (111). Sensing that this middle ground needs further definition, he adds that they occupy "a plane of evolution between that of the Neanderthal and what is known as the Grimaldi race" (111). In other words, they have come across an archaic human. The Grimaldi skull, which belonged to a European Cro-Magnon, represented the modern element while the Neanderthal subspecies, in Burroughs' mind, was a primitive dead-end. Their features, we learn, are "distinctly negroid, though their skins were white" (111). What accounts for this blend of racial traits? Campbell explains that the "Grimaldi 'Negroid' fossils, found in a cave on the Italian Riviera, were so identified mainly because their lower faces—the upper and lower jaws— projected like those of some modern … [Africans]. The projection was later found to be a distortion caused by the way the fossils had been buried" (379). Burroughs did the basic research on Grimaldi, to the point that he repeated the contradiction that workers would later resolve regarding a European skull with African facial structure. In any event, this cross-fertilization of the Neanderthal and of the Cro-Magnon had ape-like traits but stood erect. Though "very low in the scale of humanity," these creatures approached modern man because they had a language, had knowledge of fire, and wielded crude stone hatchets (111–12).

Burroughs formulates an entire hominid phylogeny in *The People That Time Forgot*, Part II of the saga. The discoveries of the Cro-Magnon, of the Neanderthal, and of *Pithecanthropus erectus*, to which we add the Piltdown hoax, pressured scientists to interrelate these finds and then subsume them under the scale of nature. It was a daunting task indeed to position these specimens logically on the vertical scale. But this is precisely what Burroughs tries to do. He therefore enumerates nine hominid sub-species and places them on a pyramidal design. From the lowest level of evolution to the highest, Burroughs lists the Ho-lu (apes), the Alu (speechless and weaponless men, one step above apes), the Bo-lu (analogous to European Neanderthals), the Sto-lu (hatchet-making cave dwellers who use fire and who are akin to *Pithecanthropus*), the Band-lu (cave-dwelling tribesmen analogous to Cro-Magnon), the Kro-lu (bow and arrow men who dwell in huts, use cooking vessels, and domesticate animals), the Galu (modern humans), and lastly the Wieroo (a race of winged Galu who live in cities, wear woven garments, and can write. Since they lack females, they must breed with kidnapped Galu women).

Finally, Burroughs introduces a dynamic element into his hierarchy: his own version of biogenetic law. This law states that the earlier stages of human embryos (and of other advanced species) resemble the embryos of ancestral species such as fish. As the embryos develop, however, they become very dissimilar. Karl Ernst von Baer (1792–1876) articulated an early version of this law after observing that embryos of different species resembled one another (Serafini 240–42). Haeckel interpreted this theory incorrectly to mean that the embryonic development of an animal (ontogeny) recapitulated the evolutionary development of the animal's ancestors (phylogeny). Burroughs adapts a similar concept to his unique idea of evolution on Caprona. Each creature on this island experiences phylosynthesis within its own lifespan: "during a single existence, [each passes] through the various stages of evolution, or at least many of them, through which the human race has passed during the countless ages since life first stirred upon a new world" (225–6). Most of these individuals evolve to higher stages although progress is unpredictable: "Some never progress beyond the Alu stage; others stop as Bo-lu, as Sto-lu, as Band-lu or as Kro-lu. The Ho-lu of the first generation may rise to become Alus; the Alus of the second generation may become Bo-lu," and so on (233).

One reason behind Burroughs' evolutionary scheme is the need to accommodate the notion of human evolution to the scale of nature. The idea of descent from primitive forms, so disturbing to many, becomes in Burroughs' fiction an ascent from the primitive to the advanced not over millions of years but within the limits of a single lifetime. Inherent in the evolutionary process that Burroughs describes is an upward, anthropocentric impulse. Accordingly, earlier forms of humanity are seen as subhuman points on this trajectory and not as unique in their own right. The anxiety generated by the prospect that Genesis could not explain human antiquity led Burroughs to assimilate phylogeny, the evolutionary history of the human race (understood here in a well-ordered paradigm), into the natural history of each individual. The adult life of the Capronian, therefore, recapitulates human phylogeny. A vestige of the Great Chain of Being persists in the Wieroo, winged men resembling angels. This is a significant clue as to Burroughs' philosophical orientation, for angels are said to exist on a plane above man but below God as a kind of link between divinity and humanity. Apparently, the Great Chain of Being is Burroughs' conceptual model for human evolution.

5

H. G. Wells's "The Grisly Folk": The Struggle for Legitimacy

H. G. Wells wrote two short stories on the subject of human pre-history ("A Story of the Stone Age" [1899] and "The Grisly Folk") and also theorized about the subject in *The Outline of History* ([1920]:63–143) and in *The Science of Life* ([1929]:1.405–24;3.796–822). Overall, his work on physical anthropology, though erudite and complex, reflects outmoded and unauthentic scientific opinions. Both his fiction and prose discourse exhibit a creative and analytical intelligence struggling, often unsuccess-fully, with illegitimate ideas about the nature and ancestry of man.

In this chapter, I will discuss the reasons behind Wells's miscon-ceptions. These reasons will emerge as we review the paleoanthropolog-ical history of the early twentieth century, along with Wells's response to it. Because his prehistoric fiction is scrupulously indebted to the work of the most renowned scientific thinkers of his times, "The Grisly Folk" reflects the fraud, erroneous interpretation, and cultural assumptions of the times. As Leon Stover has astutely observed, Wells "inaugurated the fashion in science fiction of portraying Cro-Magnon [man] as a con-quering enemy at victorious war over Neanderthal man" (318).

For Wells, the Neanderthal was an ignoble beast. In *The Outline of History* (1920), he quotes from Sir Harry Johnston's survey of the rise of modern man, an important source for his knowledge of this hominid. A famous anthropologist, colonial governor, and literary associate, Johnston provided Wells with valuable information on evolution, while another prominent spokesman for science, Sir E. Ray Lankester (director of the

Museum of Natural History), offered his expertise in ancient civilization and culture (Smith 142, 250, 252). Johnston conjectured that the remembrance of such creatures could be the basis of the ogre legend (*OH*.I.88). This opinion, which Wells endorsed, had little bearing on the fossil record inasmuch as the word "ogre" is a mythological term deriving from the Italian *orco* (for demon or monster) and from the Latin *Orcus* (for Hades or Pluto, god of the infernal world). Furthermore, an "ogre" is defined in the *OED* as "a man-eating monster, usually represented as a hideous giant." According to the fossil record, Johnston's Neanderthal "giant" was, in fact, short and stocky (Stringer [1988]:370); and even though the Paleolithic record suggests cannibalistic activities for Peking man and Yugoslavian Neanderthals (Shreeve 229), there is currently no consensus on the prevalence of this practice. Scientists such as Ashley Montagu and Pat Shipman, for instance, are doubtful that, except under extreme conditions, cannibalism was a typical feature of late Paleolithic culture ([1968]:60; [1987]:70–6). Nonetheless, in "The Grisly Folk," Wells cultivates the disturbing connection between the Neanderthal and the archetypal ogre, a devourer of humanity.

For the Neanderthals, the advent of early-modern man "was the beginning of an incessant war that could only end in extermination" (295). In Wells's prehistoric myth, early-modern humans are special creations while the Neanderthals, rather than being their taxonomic relatives, are predators that the settlers have to overcome. Wells identifies both the speaker and the reader intimately with the early-modern human protagonists ("our ancestors" [297]) as they invade the primordial forests to face their Neanderthal forerunners, described in ursine, canine, and simian terms. Although the latter are a kind of "folk," they are irredeemably "grisly" or gruesome. And although "these two sorts of men" (295) are competitors, the Neanderthal population does not occupy "the human side" where "the true men" dwell. They are obviously "not quite men." Phrases such as "grisly thing" (292, 293) or "grey monster" (293) outweigh any concessions Wells makes to the humanity of the Neanderthals. Most disturbing is the unjustified depiction of the Neanderthals as having devoured the children of early-modern man (296). Wells's grisly folk scamper like baboons (287, 291), a misrepresentation of their anatomy, and they are grouped with bears as the predators of early-modern man. As predators, the Neanderthals were stalked mercilessly as if they were lumbering cave bears (295). In failing to mention the Neanderthal's organized hunting abilities (so effective against the extinct cave bear), Wells reduces him to a solitary predator, a conclusion incompatible with the fossil record. Wells's canine imagery also departs from scientific fact as the

Neanderthal is said to gambol about on all fours, "a grey hairy wolf-like monster" (293).

To describe the relationship between hominid populations, Wells endows early-modern humans with heroic significance. After many generations, the ancestors of modern man, who had come from the south into Western Europe, defeat the last of the grisly folk (297). The imagined triumph of early-modern humans becomes the substance of heroic myth as human ingenuity and courage triumph. The speaker extols achievements that are "ours" as well: "we are lineally identical with those sun-brown painted beings who ran and fought and helped one another, the blood in our veins glowed in those fights and chilled in those fears of the forgotten past" (297). Dim recollections of this long struggle are preserved, Wells suggests, in legend and in the collective memory of mankind (297). The speaker in "The Grisly Folk" conceives of the Neanderthal as the embodiment of human fears about nature and extrudes him from human evolutionary history.

That Wells's story does not correspond to the genuine fossil record available during the early 1920s is not surprising: the scientific and public communities of the time had difficulty accepting the idea that archaic forms such as the Neanderthals pre-dated early-modern humans by 40,000 to 70,000 years (Campbell 295–6). Since many of these fossil discoveries had occurred between 1848 and 1886, replicating this record is helpful in contextualizing Wells's fiction. In 1848, the first of two Neanderthal fossils was unearthed from a Gibraltar cave (Stringer [1988]:225). A second human fossil was identified, in August 1857, as *Homo sapiens neanderthalensis*, after the Neander Valley in Germany where it had been found accidentally. These fossils provided morphological details. Shorter and more robust than modern man, Neanderthal man presented distinctive cranial features (prominent brow ridges, low sloping forehead, a protuberance at the rear of the skull, a prognathous face, no chin, and large front teeth) (Stringer [1988]:368–70). On average, his cranial capacity (ca. 1600 cubic centimeters) was as large as, if not bigger than, that of modern man. In 1868, fossil remains and implements of the Cro-Magnon man, an early-modern human who lived about 40,000 years ago, were uncovered at Les Eyzies (Dordogne, France), and further discoveries were registered in Solutré, as well as in Spain, Germany, and Eastern Europe. Two fragmentary Neanderthal skeletons were found near Spy (Belgium), in 1886, along with stone implements and the remains of extinct fauna that helped to date the European Neanderthals as having flourished sometime between 40,000 and 100,000 years ago. Despite the fossil inventory up to 1886 and even as late as the 1920s, the scientific community could not agree on the identity and significance of the Neanderthals, and Wells's writings mirror this lack of consensus. Some believed that this creature was an anthropomorphic ape, more simian than human. Others proposed that, with his pronouncedly simian features, he was an anthropoidal man. Some even thought him to have been a unique human being, related more to early-modern humans than to apes. Papers of the 1860s that help to explain Wells's thought in 1920–21 illustrate the range of opinion on the subject. Professor William King, an anatomist, conjectured that the Neander Valley specimen represented an extinct form of humanity having more in common with apes than with modern *Homo sapiens sapiens*. Others thought that the Neanderthal was not prehistoric at all. The German pathologist Rudolf Virchow (1821–1902) insisted that the specimen was really a modern man who had suffered from rickets and arthritis, conditions accounting for the unusual cranial and skeletal bones (Spencer 595; Campbell 296–7). On the other hand, Thomas Henry Huxley (1825–1895) argued that the Neanderthal was a genuine human being with archaic or "pithecoid" features. In "On Some Fossil Remains of Man" (1863), he rejects King's position: "In no sense … can the Neanderthal bones be regarded as the remains of a human being intermediate between Man and Apes"; rather, the bones illustrate "the existence of a Man whose skull may be said to revert towards the pithecoid type." But even against modern "pithecoid" skulls, "the Neanderthal cranium is by no means so isolated as it appears to be at first." Instead, Huxley suspects that this skull is "the extreme term of a series leading gradually from it to the highest and best developed of human crania" (181–3). In effect, Huxley positions the Neanderthal cranium within modern limits. The important point is that, despite the Neanderthal's archaic cranial features, Huxley believed him to have been a human being. He reiterates this thesis in "Further Remarks upon the Human Remains from Neanderthal" (1864), in which he finds no specific or generic reason for separating the Neanderthals from early-modern humanity (cited by Eisley, 273–4). Whereas many scientists of the period believed the Neanderthal specimen to have belonged to a modern individual deformed by bone disease, others such as D. Schaaffhausen believed the Neanderthal to have been an example of a prehistoric brute. In an 1858 paper, "On the Crania of the most ancient Races of Man," Schaaffhausen explains that, "the human bones and cranium from the Neanderthal exceed all the rest in these peculiarities of conformation which lead to the conclusion of their belonging to a barbarous and savage race" (123).

As late as the 1920s, Wells concurred with King and Schaaffhausen, not with his former teacher Thomas Huxley. Wells's ideas about the evolutionary place of the Neanderthal were influenced by a popular idea of him as a feral simian, what Loren Eisley calls "the wild-man" hypothesis (274–5). The Genevan scholar Karl Vogt articulated this view in *Lectures on Man* (1864), as did J. W. Dawson in *On the Antiquity of Man* (1864) (Eisley 262, 274). The latter's Neanderthal man, Eisley writes, approximates those fallen, feral creatures who inhabit "the green forests of medieval romance" (275). Dawson describes the Neanderthal man as "half-crazed, half-idiotic, cruel and strong," the sort of creature found in barbarous tribes, in the penitentiary, and on death row (Eisley 274). In effect, Dawson, following Schaaffhausen, contorted the discoveries of the Neander Valley to fit the interests of folklore.

Dawson's was not the only questionable interpretation. To explain the similarity between the 1857 discoveries and the 1886 specimens at Spy, Virchow revived his pathology thesis. Others demurred. It was now received with considerable skepticism, for it was unlikely that all of these creatures had suffered from bone diseases and were pathological moderns; moreover, artifacts and extinct fauna supported the antiquity of the remains (Campbell 296–8). In 1908, when significant remains were found near the French village of La Chapelle-aux-Saints, scientists moved the Neanderthals closer to modern man than to apes in evolutionary history. Stone implements and other skeletons found in a nearby cave at Le Moustier supported this viewpoint.

Despite these discoveries, many naturalists tenaciously resisted the possibility that the Neanderthal was a close relative of modern man. The work of one scientist, in particular, reinforced the assumption, held by theorists since William King, that Neanderthal man had more in common with apes than with man. We discussed his work in chapter 2. From 1911 to 1913, Pierre Marcellin Boule (1861–1942), French paleontologist, geologist, and chair of paleontology at the Muséum National d'Histoire, Paris (Spencer 97), tried to reconstruct the Neanderthal from skeletal remains (Campbell 298–301). Unfortunately, as I have pointed out, he misconstrued the anatomy of the feet and knee bones, falsely endowing the Neanderthal with ape-like characteristics. He also incorrectly inferred from structural features of the skull that the Neanderthal lacked human intelligence. Boule's monographs (1911–1913) promoted for decades the image of the Neanderthal as a mentally defective, anthropoidal man, and his findings influenced ideas on prehistoric humanity into the 1920s. Leon Stover correctly observes that, "The enthusiastic repulsion with which the ugliness of Neanderthal man continues to be greeted is remarkable for its staying power and eloquence" (319). This image, thanks to Boule, has proven to be an intractable stereotype.

Yet, by the turn of the century, scientific findings counteracting the stereotype continued to appear. The accurate skeletal reconstructions of the French paleontologist Camille Arambourg (1885–1969) invalidated those of Boule and demonstrated not only that Neanderthal man was fully erect but that he differed in no significant measure from modern man (Wills 153). In 1921, the same year "The Grisly Folk" was published, an important fossil was accidentally found in the Broken Hill region of Zambia (then Rhodesia). The Rhodesian man, along with ancient stone implements and extinct animal bones found with it, argued in favor of humanity's great antiquity.

The Piltdown hoax, to which I previously referred, related directly to the Neanderthal controversy because it supported the idea that prehistoric humanity (with the exception of early-modern humans) constituted an array of anthropoidal monsters very different from the lineal ancestors of man (Campbell 217–20; Spencer 452–3). In the early decades of the twentieth century, pseudo-science and fraud converged, inhibiting the pursuit of genuine prehistory. Boule's misconstruction was published at the same time as the Piltdown hoax, and their concerted effect would be felt into the 1950s (Wills 153).

The hoax began in 1911 when Charles Dawson, lawyer and antiquarian, reported that he had found skeletal remains of an early man in a gravel pit in Sussex, England (Strauss 52; Spencer 452–53). Skull fragments and a simian-like jaw were excavated from the site. In 1921, Boule concluded that Piltdown had incongruous parts—a chimpanzee-like jaw (it proved to be from an orangutan) and a humanoid skull (which was in fact human)—but deduced that the assemblage belonged to a single ancestral human (Reader 71). Because the skull had human features, and because the mandible was clearly ape-like, a number of researchers at first doubted the fossil's legitimacy. But in time the hoax gained momentum; renowned scientists such as Sir Arthur Smith Woodward (1864–1944) pronounced Piltdown to be authentic (Spencer 599). Woodward, like Boule, thought the jaw was anthropoidal and the skull human; but despite this glaring incongruity, he, too, maintained that the parts belonged to the skull of "an intermediate stage between man and ape" (Reader 65). Sir Arthur Keith (1866–1955), British anatomist and paleontologist, expressed his confidence in the authenticity of the find and in Smith Woodward's classification of it: "When we sum up all the characters which Dr. Smith Woodward has portrayed in this new form of being—the anthropoid characters of the mouth, teeth, and face, that massive and ill-filled [*sic*; ill-fitted?] skull, the simian characters of the brain and its primitive and pre-human general appearance—one feels convinced that he was absolutely justified in creating a new genus of the family Hominidae for its reception. The new genus he named Eoanthropus" (Keith 211). Incidentally, there seems to have been some miscommunication here between Woodward and Keith with respect to the skull, for Woodward believed the skull qualified as human since its cranial capacity was 1070 cubic centimeters; but Keith, for whatever reason, called the brain "simian." Other respected professionals unequivocally endorsed Piltdown's authenticity. Of *Eoanthropus Dawsoni* (as the find was so named), Arles Hrdlička (1869–1943) wrote in 1913 that, "it is no longer possible to regard the jaw as that of a chimpanzee or any other anthropoid ape ... it is the jaw either of a human precursor or a very early man" (50). The "wild-man" hypothesis appeared to have been vindicated—at least until 1953, when J. S. Weiner and Le Gros Clark of Oxford extruded the Piltdown assemblage from the human family. The skull, they unequivocally determined, had come from a modern individual and the jaw from a chimpanzee. All of this material had been planted at the site.

In 1920 Wells, once again, agreed with the wrong authority, this time with anthropologists such as Hrdlička. To make matters worse, he failed to heed the warning of Sir E. Ray Lankester who, in a letter of 1918, had advised him against mentioning the Piltdown Man since its authenticity was being questioned by so many in the scientific community (Smith 252).

In his historical survey of apes, sub-men, and men, however, Wells confidently observes that *Eoanthropus* (or "Dawn man") is "a creature still ascending only very gradually from the sub-human" (*OH*.I.72). Wells also thought the cranial fragments were archaic rather than contemporary: "It is a thick skull ... and it has a brain capacity intermediate between that of Pithecanthropus [the Java man] and man" (*OH*.I.72). Counterfeit animal artifacts at the site fooled Wells, along with contemporary professionals (*OH*.I.72). What should have been identified as a chimpanzee jaw is, for Wells, a sub-human fossil: "It is extraordinarily like that of a chimpanzee, but Sir Arthur Keith [anatomist and paleontologist (1866–1955)] assigns it, in his *Antiquity of Man* (1915), to the skull with which it is found. It is, as a jaw-bone, far less human in character than the jaw of the much more ancient *Homo Heidelbergensis*, but the teeth are in some respects more like those of living men" (*OH*.I.72). Wells should be credited for having consulted the most authoritative opinions on the subject.

Actually, the chimpanzee's teeth had been abraded and stained to have the look of remains from an archaic hominid. During the 1950s, Dr. J. S. Weiner determined, through X-ray examination and fluorine analysis, that the lower jaw and canine tooth were actually those of a "modern anthropoid ape, deliberately altered so as to resemble fossil specimens" (Strauss 50). The investigators determined that "the faking of the mandible and canine [was] so extraordinarily skillful, and the perpetration of the hoax ... was so entirely unscrupulous and inexplicable, as to find no parallel in the history of paleontological discovery" (Weiner, Oakley, Le Gros Clark [Heizer 36]). According to Wells's paraphrase of Keith, Eoanthropus "was a member of a number of species of sub-human running apes of more than ape-like intelligence, and if it was not on the line royal it was ... a very close collateral" (*OH*.I.72). From all the conflicting theories, Wells erroneously (although logically) inferred that the Neanderthal man co-existed with, and was a correlative of, *Eoanthropus* (*OH*.I.75).

One cannot blame Wells for accepting the authenticity of Piltdown since the authorities whom he consulted had done so as well. But how did Wells use this information fictively? Although, in *The Outline of History*, he distinguishes between the two forms, in "The Grisly Folk," he includes all archaic hominids under the Neanderthal taxon, calling the feral hominids in the story "Mousterians" or "Neandertalers" (286) when, in fact, the creatures seem to be incarnations of the Piltdown assemblage. Wells, it appears, perfunctorily grouped all forms of archaic humanity under the Neanderthal nomenclature, obscuring the latter's resemblance to early-modern humans; and then he staged a territorial conflict between the two groups for dramatic, mythological, and cultural effect.

I detect Wells's taxonomic confusion in his assessment of the relationship between the Neanderthals and early-modern humans. In one particular passage, the *Eoanthropus* problem disoriented him. Alluding to findings at Krapina (in Croatia), at the Neander Valley, and at Spy, he states unequivocally that this creature is human but then says that *Homo sapiens neanderthalensis* has become "a quite passable human being" (*OH*.I.75). At this point his description is fairly accurate, but the closer he moves Neanderthal man to the modern human lineage, the more unsure he becomes with this decision perhaps because this creature's close proximity to modern man controverts the received authority of Boule and of Virchow. Or perhaps Wells recalled Lankester's suspicions about Piltdown Man. Consequently, what was definitely human devolves rapidly to a "passable human being" and, finally, to a creature "not quite of the human species" (*OH*.I.73). One source of Wells's confusion is paleocraniometry. Although the Neanderthal brain is "as big as ours," he writes, its owner is not only intellectually inferior to modern man but "simpler" and "lower." Wells is reading the skull phrenologically when he assumes that the cranial differences between the Neanderthals and early-modern humans constitute definitive proof that the former belong to a disparate evolutionary line (*OH.I.76*). This belief overshadows both *The Outline of History* and "The Grisly Folk."

The nefarious effect of the Piltdown hoax on paleoanthropological thought, reflected in Wells's 1921 fiction, should not be underestimated. John Reader and Stephen Jay Gould explain that the hoax corroborated racist theory. In the first place, Piltdown vindicated chauvinistic assumptions about Anglo-Saxons and white Europeans. As John Reader explains, the Piltdown specimens suggested that mankind already had a large brain by the beginning of the Pleistocene Epoch, one million years ago. That was an important assumption: since large-brained archaic man existed that long ago and was by virtue of that trait the direct ancestor of *Homo sapiens sapiens*, the Javan and Neanderthal fossils, with their anthropoidal features, could be conveniently expelled from the human lineage. Java man could also be dismissed as a small-brained offshoot, and the large-brained Neanderthal could be explained away as a similar dead-end. In the 1920s and 1930s, Piltdown would therefore become the standard for the primacy of the Cro-Magnon man over other forms thought more primitive (Reader 73). Such a position could be used to establish the veracity of the scale of nature and to refute the heretical idea that man, instead of being created immutably by divine fiat, had descended from primitive forebears.

The racial and cultural implications of Piltdown explain Wells's dichotomous portrayal of ancient man, the evil beast (Neanderthal man) and the heroic pioneer (Cro-Magnon man). Gould points out that, in 1913, a large brain was correlated to high intelligence and was thought, by anthropologists, to have preceded all other alterations in the human body ([1980]:116–17). According to this view, genuine human ancestors had large brains and ape-like bodies. Actually, the reverse was proving to be true, according to the fossil record. But the Piltdown find reversed this trend in favor of those who subscribed to the scale of nature. With its human brain and ape-like jaw and bones, Piltdown vindicated conservative evolutionary theory. Big-brained Piltdown also reinforced racial assumptions. In the 1930s and 1940s, after Peking man had been found in strata approximately as deep as that in which Piltdown was found (suggesting their concurrence), phyletic diagrams began to appear asserting the greater antiquity and superiority of the white race over all others (Gould [1980]:116–17). To many, this was logical because Peking man, an ancestor of modern-day Chinese, had a brain that was two-thirds smaller than that of Piltdown. Piltdown, however, lived in England, so it followed that Englishmen were the progenitors of the white race and that dark-skinned people derived from *erectus*. Some concluded, writes Gould, that "whites crossed the threshold to full humanity long before other people" ([1980]:117). No doubt this state of affairs could account in part for the imperialistic exaltation of early European man in the "Grisly Folk." Early man was an Englishman—or a close relative.

During the early 1920s, Wells's idea of prehistoric humanity reflected wrong-headed science, specifically the kind that Virchow, Boule, the Piltdown forgers, Vogt, and J. W. Dawson cultivated. Each had his own motivation, preconceived idea, and approach. But these lines converged in the early twentieth century, reaching their apogee in 1920, when Wells renewed his interest in human prehistory. Had he remained true to Huxley's thought, one can argue that he would have produced a more consistent view of Neanderthal man during the early 1920s. For Wells, early-modern man had originated in England and was, therefore, ordained in cultural and natural history as the exemplary imperialist.

Although inconsistent science distorted Wells's fiction in 1920, the same cannot be said of "A Story of the Stone Age" (1899), a work that though slighted among the corpus of Wells's "biological S[cience] F[iction]" (Mullen 225, 227) is a worthy forerunner of modern works in the genre (Smith 74). Written before Boule's work, the "wild-man" hypothesis, or the Piltdown hoax (but not before Vogt, Schaaffhausen, and others), "Stone Age" demonstrates that Wells had indeed consulted reputable scientific reports on the Neanderthal in 1899, blending this material into his fiction. His Neanderthal physiology is accurate (Uya the Cunning is "beetle-browed," "prognathous," and "lank-armed" [362]). "Stone Age" leads me to believe that, in 1899, Wells had little doubt about the intelligence of Neanderthal man. The details of his tool manufacture are well represented: the protagonist, Ugh-lomi, fashions a stone axe after fixing a flint to a stick (373). As the tribe prepares to hunt a lion, its members industriously hack away at spears and throwing stones to make an array of weapons. A dream reveals Ugh-lomi's technical virtuosity as he envisions a serrated club made from hacked alder wood into which lion's teeth and claws have been hammered (411). On yet another point "Stone Age" demonstrates scientific consistency. From 1856 to the publication of "Stone Age," scientists had speculated on the importance of rituals in Neanderthal life. Of these speculations, Wells was clearly aware: anthropomorphism, reincarnation, and propitiatory ritual each have a place in his story. Uya, the shaman, possesses a "white Fire Stone" that none but he dare touch (367); the ability to kindle fire is inherent in the office of shaman. Ugh-lomi animistically exhorts "Brother Fire" for assistance

(380); his deceased rival, Uya, is believed to have been reincarnated as the lion terrorizing the clan and exacting revenge (396, 400); the clan considers sacrificing Ugh-lomi to appease this lion-spirit (410). "A Story of the Stone Age" corresponds more accurately to the accumulating and irrefutable evidence drawn from the fossils in aggregate.

In *The Science of Life* (1929), Wells and his collaborators also avoid the "wild-man" characterization. By this time, anthropological theory reliant on the fossil record and on sound investigative methods had begun to make headway against the unauthentic and erroneous scientific influences of the early 1920s. Another possible reason for the revision is that Sir Julian Huxley (1887–1975), a distinguished biologist, was responsible for some 70 percent of the writing of this work (Mullen 256). Great discoveries of the Neanderthals and of more archaic beings continued to be made in that decade. In 1925, Raymond Dart (b. 1893), a South African paleontologist, discovered the "Taung" child, which he named *Australopithecus africanus*, literally "southern ape" (Spencer 152; Tattersall [1993]: 82–3; Grine 67–8). In 1926 the Devil's Tower quarry on the Rock of Gibraltar yielded a child's skull: its large brain size revealed its taxon as Neanderthal (Stringer [1988]:225). And, in 1927, the Canadian anatomist Davidson Black (1884–1934), while excavating Dragon Bone Hill near Peking, found bone fragments and teeth of "Peking man," a human being (sub-species *erectus*) resembling Java man (Campbell 68–9, 210–13; Tattersall [1993]:104–5, 107). The accumulating fossil evidence of creatures even older than the Neanderthals moved the latter closer to modern man than to any other group on the evolutionary scale.

With this new knowledge, the authors of *The Science of Life* reconsider the ritualistic possibilities of Neanderthal culture:

> Other species of bygone men ... were left to moulder where they died, like animals; but the Neanderthalers laid out some at least of their dead in their caves and put tools and implements beside them and buried them, presumably because they did not believe life was wholly ended, and so put these things for the use of the departed if and when he or she awoke again. It is rash to guess too precisely what ideas led to these interments. They had ideas and doubts about death, no doubt, that resulted in burial [413].

Apparently, the authors knew about sites in Drachenloch and in southern France (Campbell 346–8; Tattersall [1993] 126–7; Shreeve 52–4, 90–1). From 1856 to 1970, scientists attributed a religious sensibility to the Neanderthals whose rites were thought to have been intimately associated with the central activity of hunting. The so-called "bear cult" is the most well-known example of his hunting magic. In the Swiss Alps, from 1917 to 1923, a German archaeologist, Emil Bachler, excavated the cave of Drachenloch. In its interior, he found a stone chest containing seven bear skulls, ritually arranged in wall niches. An early find in the cave of La Chapelle-aux-Saints also suggested the Neanderthals' belief in an after-life. An ancient hunter had been laid out in a shallow trench and provisioned with animal bones and flint, presumably to be used in the after-life. In 1912, Neanderthal graves at La Ferrassie also supported this hypothesis (Campbell 353).

In *The Science of Life*, the authors judiciously reprise the idea of inter-breeding: "It is pure guesswork whether Homo neanderthalensis in any region interbred or did not interbreed with Homo sapiens" (1440). To describe the interaction between hominid populations, Wells et al. point to a more fluid model. Later Paleolithic man, they conjecture, varied widely from region to region, with "strongly marked," more easily-classified types (e.g., Cro-Magnon man) appearing under special condi-tions, and suggesting genetic intermixture. At this late juncture in evolutionary history, early-modern humans and Neanderthals, though they may have clashed, may also have interbred with and learned from each other. Wells proposes that two interactive modes, "imitation and pre-cept," brought the two groups into closer accord and may have initiated further genetic variation (1440).

"The Grisly Folk" promulgates a distorted image of prehistoric humanity not because Wells ignored or misinterpreted the predominant scientific opinions but because, in 1921, the prevailing authorities were dominated by fraud, preconceived notions, and erroneous interpretations. Free of mythological contaminants, the writings of 1899 and of 1929 cor-respond to scientific opinions grounded on harder evidence. On the sub-ject of human evolution, one could justifiably conclude that Wells's writings, whether historical, analytical, or fictional, are indices to current scientific speculations and to the debates they ignited.

In the final analysis, it appears that Wells never revised the opinions set forth in "The Grisly Folk." Comments in the Conclusion to *A Short History of the World*, a revised edition of the 1945 work, contradict the incisive survey of paleoanthropology in *The Science of Life*. In Chapter Eight of *A Short History*, Wells reiterates the gross inaccuracies of "The Grisly Folk," but now one cannot blame his errors on the scientific milieu. He begins by grouping pre-humans (probably *erectus*) correctly under the superfamily Hominidae, but his intemperate rhetoric precludes objective commentary: the hominids responsible for "Chellean" tool industry are nothing more than "great quasi-human lout-beasts" who "hunted and killed" with "uncouth cries." Their clumsy hands "battered out the Chellean implements" (*Last Books*, 62–3). The Chellean industrialists whom Wells derides lived from 1.5 million to 200,000 years ago and are believed to have produced large bifacially flaked, ovoid tools, as well as flint hand axes, and they probably lived as hunter-gatherers. From 1945 to this very day, our knowledge of the ecology and behavior of the Chellean industrialists (now called Acheulian)—of these "quasi-human lout-beasts"—is speculative, at best (Potts 3–5). So what are we to infer from Wells's revival, in 1945, of the false dichotomy between brutish ancestors and auspicious moderns? It certainly does not reflect his ignorance of the subject. It may reflect an unresolved conflict in his mind about the nature of prehistoric humanity and about their modern descendants.

6

Lester Del Rey's "The Day Is Done" and the Tasmanian Analogue

Lester Del Rey's short story "The Day Is Done" (1939) dramatizes the final days of an enfeebled Neanderthal whose world the Cro-Magnon man invades. In this work, the author treats two interrelated themes: the conflict between these human sub-species and the roots of discrimination, manifested in their enmity.

To explore these issues in depth, I have subdivided this chapter into two parts. In the first, I compare Del Rey's version of late–Paleolithic human history to contemporaneous discoveries in paleoanthropology. According to Del Rey, this epoch in human history was characterized by the rise and fall of parallel cultures: that of the dying Neanderthals and that of the ascendant Cro-Magnons. In part two, I connect the fictional relationship between the Neanderthals and the Cro-Magnons to that of the Tasmanians and the English colonists of Tasmania. The plight of Vivienne Trucanini, the last of the Tasmanian Aborigines who died in 1876, is analogous to Hwoogh's fictional situation. Despite important studies by Robert Travers, David Michael Davies, and Matthew Kneale, the unique history of the Tasmanians is not well known.

The parallel between the two groups is cogent. Both the Neanderthals and the Tasmanians succumbed to the physical, psychological, cultural, and genetic hegemony of the newcomers (Cro-Magnon man and English colonists, respectively), despite instances of gratuitous kindness and of efforts at co-existence. The heroic dignity of Hwoogh is intensified as he declines: the more intense his isolation, the more human he appears;

59

and the more human he appears, the more one questions the behavior of Del Rey's Cro-Magnon. As for the fate of the Tasmanian survivors up to 1876, their story remains an ugly footnote in the history of South Pacific anthropology.

Paleoanthropological Background and Fictional Foreground

The decade of the 1930s was a prodigious time to write about prehistory. From 1929 to 1934, as Christopher Stringer recounts in an informative article, excavations in a cave site at Mugharet-es-Skhūl, on Mount Carmel (Israel), produced parietal skeletons of an adult and a child (523). The bones appeared to have been intentionally burned. Originally, they were dated as early as the late Pleistocene but now have been dated as being 40,000 years old. Over the period of excavation, a total of seven adults and three children were retrieved. Most impressive were three nearly complete adult skulls and some long bones. Workers in the 1930s conjectured, on the basis of these specimens, that the Neanderthals had been in the process of evolving into early-modern man. Further evaluation has suggested that the Skhūl remains possibly belonged to hybrids of Neanderthals and of early-modern humans. Skhūl humans, such as the robust early-modern types living in western Asia, retained some archaic features from their ancestors. Some even think that the Skhūl specimens represented the ancestors of the European Cro-Magnon man (Stringer [1988]:523).

During the 1930s, the Skhūl team was also working at another site at Tabun, a cave on Mount Carmel. A female skeleton and a male mandible were found there and recently dated at ca. 50,000 years old. The female skull which is small (1300 milliliters in volume) exhibits strong brow development and the kind of pubic-bone morphology associated with the Neanderthals. The classification of the male mandible, however, has remained unclear. In 1931, a third discovery of Neanderthal specimens occurred near the Solo River, in Ngandong, eastern Java. From 1931 to 1933, the remains of twelve individuals were located. One skull, reconstructed from a cranial cap, held a volume between 1035 to 1225 milliliters. Whereas some believed they belonged to Neanderthals, presently scientists are considering the possibility that the specimens are either early forms of archaic *Homo sapiens sapiens* or later forms of *erectus*.

The fossil evidence I describe above strengthens the theory that Neanderthals evolved into early-modern humans, generically known under the western European name of Cro-Magnon man. At the time that Del

Rey was writing his story, three theories hoped to explain the historical relationship between the co-extensive hominids, Neanderthal and Cro-Magnon: (1) some Neanderthals evolved into modern human beings; (2) all Neanderthals evolved into modern human beings; or (3) all Neanderthals became extinct and were replaced by modern man who evolved from "an unknown genetic stock" (Campbell 366). The period in question, quite brief by geological standards, ranged from 50,000 or 30,000 to 20,000 years ago. According to Bernard G. Campbell, the physical features of Neanderthals and of early-modern humans in this period could be positioned on a continuum. At some point on this continuum, statistical evidence further suggests, an evolutionary threshold between Neanderthal and Cro-Magnon man was crossed, not abruptly through sudden extinction, but through the accretion of nearly imperceptible anatomical changes. Campbell deduces that the features of most Neanderthals gradually became those of modern people (371). The finds at Skhūl suggest that much the same was true for prehistoric humanity in the Middle East. Those in Eastern Europe, at Předmosti, and at Sipka in Czechoslovakia, also point to this possibility. And those in Southeast Asia bolster this theory. A possible evolutionary linkage was established between Solo man, an early Javan Neanderthal, and most ancient fossils of Australian Aborigines. Although transitional specimens in eastern and in southern Africa were lacking, one found at Florisbad had Neanderthal features (Campbell 371). Furthermore, there are scientists who believe that the African Neanderthals were actually the first to develop into modern forms (372).

In Western Europe, during the 1930s, no true fossil intermediate between local Neanderthals and the Cro-Magnons had as yet been found. Thus, in 1939, Del Rey had a wonderfully inventive opportunity but, unfortunately, one that was never realized since the story was not anchored in its scientific and historical context. Although the coming of Cro-Magnon man, for Del Rey, means the end of the Neanderthals, his portrayal of the relationship between the two hominid groups does not correspond to what had come to light paleontologically. Despite the Mount Carmel discoveries, Del Rey subscribes to the contentious theory that Cro-Magnon supplanted Neanderthal man. He makes this clear, for example, when he writes that Neanderthal reproductive rates decreased as Cro-Magnon populations increased, a decline the speaker attributes to the arrival of modern humans (12).

Del Rey points out that the beginning of the end commenced for the Neanderthals even before the "Talkers" had arrived at the end of the Fourth and final Glaciation of the Pleistocene, 35,000 to 50,000 years ago (Campbell 350). According to the narrator, the Neanderthals enjoyed a brief resurgence after the Fourth Glaciation. Unlike the Cro-Magnons who, at that time, were migrating from other regions, Neanderthal society had become relatively static as its members regrouped in geographical niches. Consequently, "the Talkers took more and more land, and [Hwoogh's] people retreated and diminished before them." Eventually Hwoogh's father disclosed that "their little band in the valley was all that was left, and that this was the only place on the great flat earth where Talkers seldom came" (13). Hwoogh recalls, however, that the articulate Cro-Magnons behaved "as if they owned the earth" (13).

Del Rey indicates that he researched the subject generally, but, on one point, he commits a serious error, assuming that the outward shape of the skull or even an inner cast of its anatomy, called an endocranial cast, can tell us anything definitive about the vocal capacity of a hominid (a subject discussed at greater length in the following chapter). Currently, it is recognized that our knowledge of the neuro-circuitry of the Neanderthal frontal lobe is severely limited since all we have to judge from are reconstructed skulls and molds of their inner surfaces. To assume, therefore, that a retreating forehead and bulging browridges are reliable indices of language capacity is to practice a form of phrenology, a pseudo-science claiming to draw conclusions about mental faculties and character traits from the shape of the human skull (Finger 32–6). The Austrian anatomist Franz Joseph Gall (1758–1828) developed this theory in the first decade of the nineteenth century (Finger 303–4). Collaborating with his student, Johann Caspar Spurzheim (1776–1832), Gall studied the nervous system and brain extensively, and, from 1810 to 1819, they published their findings in a four-volume work and atlas. Gall made a number of important discoveries, one of which was that the white matter of the brain consisted of fibers. He also promulgated the doctrine that mental processes could be localized in specific locations of the brain. Today, phrenology and its concomitant theories are dismissed as quackery. From the 1960s onward, the focus of debate concerning Neanderthal speech has centered not on the brain but rather on the anatomy of the vocal tract, from which much has been learned through reconstructive and comparative techniques; yet even from this perspective, no consensus about the thinking processes of prehistoric man has as yet been established among paleoanthropologists. But Del Rey is partially accurate when he writes that Hwoogh can only make a sign for horses because "The shape of his jaw and the attachments of his tongue, together with the poorly developed left frontal lobe of his brain, made speech rudimentary, [so] he supplemented his glottals and labials with motions that Keyoda understood well enough" (15). Of the three features cited (jaw, tongue, and brain), the tongue attachments (scientists reputedly have proven) are what prevented the Neanderthal from speaking.

Cro-Magnon culture and technology, closely intertwined aspects of their lifestyle, outwardly manifest this hominid's intellectual and morphological superiority to the Neanderthal man. The Cro-Magnon migrants, whose language capacity annoys Hwoogh, create habitations out of the raw wilderness while the Neanderthals who are incapable of articulate speech must live in cave shelters. Significantly, Del Rey's Talkers use animal skins and make shelters out of them (13). Moreover, they situate their camps on the downside of hills for shelter against cave predators and the elements.

The newcomers also possess a systematic religion. Hwoogh who seems to have adopted their solar worship believes that this deity favors the newcomers over his people. For this reason, he correlates the decline of his people to the "strength of the sun god" (14). Del Rey may have been implying that the gloom of the Fourth Glaciation had given way to more sunlight, a condition favoring the Cro-Magnons who would develop into agriculturalists (14). Their weapons are especially effective against predators (13). They help themselves to the best game, leaving Hwoogh to lament that his band had to accept the humiliation of the Cro-Magnons' intrusion into their territory. Finally, Hwoogh's band had to resort to "begging and stealing" (13).

Hwoogh's predicament as the sole survivor of a dying sub-species is tragic. In an interchange with Legoda, the compassionate Cro-Magnon shaman, he learns of a small Neanderthal family that had lived in the vicinity three years before. Though the Cro-Magnon people supported them, and though the Neanderthals were traditionally hunters, they died inexplicably. And even though this nuclear family did not lack sustenance, "they were thin and scrawny, too lazy to hunt." As far as Legoda and his tribe know, Hwoogh is the last of his kind (20). The workings of natural selection and the signs of impending extinction in regard to the Neanderthals, though concepts beyond Legoda's ken, still move him to reflect that Hwoogh's people "die too easily ... no sooner do we find them and try to help them than they cease hunting and become beggars. And they lose interest in life, sicken and die. I think your [Hwoogh's] gods must be killed off by our stronger ones" (20). In a sense this is true, for the Neanderthals succumb not to the direct attack of Cro-Magnon man but to a kind of cultural hegemony: that is, to the newcomers' obtrusive presence, large-scale hunting practices, sprawling settlements, and cultural dominance, factors marginalizing the cave-dwelling Neanderthals and eclipsing their rudimentary technology and culture. Though the Neanderthals try to keep up, and though they are encouraged to participate in Cro-Magnon life, they are simply too disadvantaged morphologically. Understanding that they have been marginalized as a sub-species, they are unable to prevent their way of life from stagnating.

Hwoogh embodies the Neanderthal ethos with all of its evolutionary deficits. The physiological limitations of the Neanderthals are poignantly exemplified, for example, when Legoda introduces Hwoogh to the bow and arrow, a new invention that can slay animals at a distance. Hwoogh whose fingers are large and maladroit is unable to wield this new weapon (19–20). There are two aspects to the Neanderthal's disability: the first is that he is anatomically maladapted; the second, more insidious factor is that Hwoogh has given up mentally. Resenting the Cro-Magnon incursion and their unprecedented ingenuity, he grumbles that they have killed "all the good game" (19). To Hwoogh, the Cro-Magnons seem to overhunt; but, in all likelihood, they are able to procure an abundance of game quite easily because they are technically efficient hunters, and because they require more meat to feed their growing population. Unlike the Neanderthals who probably engage in limited hunting forays the Cro-Magnons are migrant hunters who pursue herds and who encamp in uncharted regions. The Neanderthals who do not have the ability to build sophisticated weaponry and mobile shelters are not nearly as itinerant.

Del Rey does not imagine a world in which the Cro-Magnon people are benevolent conquerors. But I get the sense that they are exercising a kind of manifest destiny in western Europe, and they seem to be fulfilling their evolutionary destiny unknowingly. Although they tolerate and even support the indigenous Neanderthals, the latter remain segregated in caves and undergo attrition because their genetic endowment does not allow for accommodation to a changing world. A more nefarious aspect of the history between Neanderthal and Cro-Magnon man emerges at several points in the story. Though the shaman, Legoda, and the Cro-Magnon cast-off, Keyoda, treat Hwoogh affectionately, others resent and even detest him. A sense of cultural guilt rather than of unadulterated compassion motivates Legoda. He and his people "owe [Hwoogh's] kind some pay—this was his hunting ground when we were pups, straggling into this far land" (16). But his mate and others, especially the youngest generation of the tribe, have other feelings towards the indigenous people. The children of the village actually enjoy Hwoogh-baiting which they indulge in against their parents' instructions. Breaking into Hwoogh's cave one day, girls smear his face with mud while boys "ransacked the cave and tore at his clothes" (22). The chief's eldest son,

Kechaka, reminds his friends that there will be trouble if the Elders find out that they have been bothering the old Neanderthal. But they ignore his warning. The xenophobic impulse is too strong to resist, so they persecute Hwoogh, denying his humanity on the basis that he is different, foreign. Thus, one child states: "He isn't a man, anyway, but an animal; see the hair on his body! Toss old Ugly Face in the river, clean up his cave, and hide these treasures. Who's to know?" (22). The children beat, bind, and nearly drown him.

Although Hwoogh manages to get free, he dies from his ordeal, despite the nursing efforts of Legoda and Keyoda. Hwoogh, in the end, comes to terms with his life and with the extinction of his kind. His personal and ethnic dignity are irreducible, for he realizes that enslavement is unacceptable. His alienation is deeply felt. Not only is he removed from his forebears, but he is also separated from the culture and genetic pool from which he sprang.

Detached from its scientific moorings in the 1930s, "The Day Is Done" works out the possibilities of one prominent Neanderthal and Cro-Magnon theory: that early-modern man drove the precursor to extinction through competition and conflict. This scenario permits Del Rey to cultivate the persona of Hwoogh who embodies a dying breed heroically. He becomes heroic not because he physically resists those who disenfranchise his people, but because he defies an inimical environment and Cro-Magnon invaders.

There is a symbolic dimension to the story. Del Rey was obviously concerned with racism, as well as with the treatment of the elderly and of the physically challenged. His point is that the propensity to marginalize, to dehumanize, and eventually to murder the alien—whether in death camps or under seemingly benign environmental conditions—is a human trait. That the story appeared in 1939 is significant. In the autumn of that year, Nazi barbarism against the Jews began in earnest under the leadership of Hans Frank and Arthur Seyss-Inquart (Shirer 659–65).

The Tasmanian Analogue

The Tasmanian Aborigines' relationship with white colonists and that allegedly existing between the Neanderthals and the Cro-Magnons have much in common fundamentally. A number of influential scientists propagated the idea that the Tasmanians were throwbacks to ancestral forms of man. Among them was François Péron (1775–1810), a young physician, anatomist, and zoologist, and a student of Cuvier. Péron left his studies in 1800 to join the Baudin expedition to the South Pacific

(Stocking 32). Interested in testing natural selection experimentally, Péron compared the physical strength of Tasmanians and Europeans. He believed that the Tasmanians occupied the bottom rung on the ladder of civilization while Europeans occupied the highest rung (32–3). Governed by this scheme (that is, by the scale of nature), he tried to show that the islanders were constitutionally weaker than Europeans because they were poor and socially downcast. In addition to these conclusions, he enunciated other assumptions based on limited ethological information, one of which was the preposterous idea that because the Tasmanians were not promiscuous, they, like animals, must have mating seasons. An accumulation of skewed findings led Péron to conclude that the Tasmanians were unable to ascend on the scale of civilization and that their lowly and static position meant that they were destined to be wiped out. Because they could not adapt to the environment that English colonialism had radically altered, they were doomed, and their fate was justified in natural terms.

In 1856, the French pathologist, neurosurgeon, and anthropologist Paul Broca (1824–1880) reiterated Péron's idea that the Tasmanians were not truly human and were members of another species. He based this conclusion on the belief that the children of Tasmanian and Germanic unions were presumably infertile; hence, there was a great likelihood that the Tasmanians belonged to a different species altogether (or so went the argument) (Stocking 48). The failure of the Tasmanians to adapt to white civilization and their rapid descent reinforced the notion, in the minds of writers like Franklin Giddings, that the islanders were inherently inferior and that their elimination as an ethnic group was inevitable (48).

The opinions cited above provide some sense of what the scientific establishment thought of dark-skinned people such as the Tasmanians. But humane perspectives offer some contrast. We need only consider several of Captain James Cook's entries in his *Journal* to see the Tasmanians as human beings, whose collective image appears less convex in the mirror of pre-evolutionary biology. In January 1777, Cook landed on Van Diemen's Land to procure hay for his livestock and to replenish his wood supply. His shore party met a group of islanders whom Cook describes as "mild Tasmanian negroids," suggesting that they are peaceful and dignified. Their women, most notably, "rejected the advances of some of the English 'gentlemen'" (206) who obviously took them for attractive human beings and not for animals. When the indignant Tasmanians rebuffed the British, Cook marveled at their behavior, realizing that they were highly insulted and not to be pressed (208). As it was soon learned, civilized behavior, strong family loyalties, a monogamous tradition, and not Péron's claim of periodicity, explained the Tasmanians' rebuff of the English "gentlemen" in Cook's party. The testimony of contemporaries, such as Robert Thirkell, who lived among them, and of George Arthur, the lieutenant governor appointed to drive them out, confirmed Cook's initial impression that they were, indeed, a noble and inoffensive people (Montagu [1976]:168).

Captain Cook's journal entry of 27 January describes the Tasmanians accurately. On that day, a group of men approached the shore party, once again with poise and dignity. One can only imagine how Cook's shore party felt as the visitors came near:

> They were quite naked & wore no ornaments, except the large punctures or ridges raised on the skin, some in straight and others in curved lines, might be reckoned as such; they were of the common Stature but rather slender; their skin was black and also their hair, which was as Woolly as any Native of Guinea, but they were not distinguished by remarkable thick lips nor flat Noses, on the contrary their features were far from disagreeable; they had pretty good eyes and their teeth were tolerable even but very dirty; most of them had their hair and beards anointed with red ointment and some had their faces painted with the same composition ... [207].

Cook had little doubt that these natives were dignified human beings as one gathers from the physical description. Other notable features convey the idea that Cook was sensitive to the nuances of native culture: the Tasmanians, for example, practiced scarification and "anoint[ed]" themselves with body paint, both of which indicate a symbolic and ritualistic sense—a suspicion about the Tasmanians Sir James Frazer would later confirm (294). These were not wretched savages, by any means. For this reason, no doubt, Cook sympathized with them in their sufferings under colonial rule.

Darwin's opinion of the Tasmanians is intriguing but ambivalent. On the one hand, in his *Journal of Researches* (later entitled *The Voyage of the Beagle* [1839]), he calls the removal of the Aborigines from Van Diemen's Land "a great advantage." On the other hand, he qualifies this statement, referring to their deportation as "cruel" but unavoidable. Darwin acknowledges that, ever since the British had colonized the island, the whites had abused the blacks, creating enmity between the two racial groups. Subsequently, however, the blacks committed a succession of robberies, burnings, and homicides (presumably of white settlers), so the government enacted martial law in 1830. The only way of avoiding the "utter destruction" of the indigenous people, it was decided, was for the colonial government to segregate the native population on nearby Flinders' Island. Over the course of thirty years, Cook's mild-mannered and dignified people would become thieves, arsonists, and murderers. The struggle with the colonists Darwin aptly calls a "train of evil and its consequences," having originated in "the infamous conduct" of the British (387). Of this fact, Darwin had little doubt.

The problem of aboriginal unrest, Darwin recounts, was ruthlessly solved, in 1830, when the "entire race" was to be captured. The means of capture, modeled after "the great hunting matches in India," was designed to drive animals out of the bush: "a line was formed reaching across the island, with the intention of driving the natives into a cul-de-sac on Tasman's peninsula" (387). Although this plan failed, due to the evasive tactics of the Tasmanians, eventually the weary natives surrendered. Thirteen did so initially and then a majority was induced to be deported voluntarily in 1835. According to one of Darwin's sources, 120 Tasmanians were detained; however, by 1842, the exiled population on Flinders' Island amounted to only 54 individuals (388). At the time, it was difficult to account for this alarming decline in population inasmuch as aboriginal families in the interior of New South Wales were prospering and having "swarms of children." By 1843, according to Darwin's demographic source, only fourteen of the exiles remained.

The subsequent decline of the Tasmanians sufficiently intrigued Darwin to take up the issue in *The Descent of Man* (1874). In this text, Darwin again relies on John Bonwick's (1817–1906) historical and demographic writings, among which are the *Daily Life of the Tasmanians* and *The Last of the Tasmanians; or, the black war of Van Diemen's Land.* Darwin surveyed their descent, thirteen years after the last native had died (191–2). From the Dutch colonization in 1642, when seven to twenty thousand individuals populated Van Diemen's Land, to 1861, the population had been virtually wiped out. A combination of factors, including direct British attacks and less tangible environmental, psychological, and social causes, were responsible. Darwin reiterates that after the infamous "hunt" of 1830, which captured 120 people, the entire population was sent to Flinders' Island in 1832 (191) (1835, in the *Journal*), an environment quite similar to Van Diemen's Land. The Tasmanians, healthy at the time of their departure, were allegedly not mistreated, and the new location was thought to favorable to them (191). Despite these auspicious conditions, by 1834, the population had been halved to 111 individuals; by 1835, it declined to about 100; and by 1843, to 68. In order to improve their lives and to stimulate procreation, the colonists moved them again, this time to Oyster Cove in the southern part of Tasmania, presumably an even better locale than Flinders' Island. But that did not help: by 1847, there were 46 left, the last one dying in 1861 (*sic*; 1876).

Like Darwin, H. G. Wells struggled with racist and humanitarian sentiments with respect to the Tasmanians, and his intellectual (and ethical) struggles are noteworthy, given his interest in anthropology. He published several important but rather ambivalent comments on them. As early as 1898, for example, Wells would compare Martian hegemony over the human race, in *The War of the Worlds*, to that of the British colonists over the Tasmanians (55). The Martians who needed to escape a dying world and to find a new source of food (with man serving that purpose) occupy the moral high ground in this comparison. From a biological perspective, the Martians are natural predators whereas the British colonists are wholly unjustified in their conduct towards native peoples. Territory was presumably not the issue since the Tasmanians occupied small villages and, at the very outset, they and the English co-existed peacefully. Contempt for the dark-skinned natives, which contrived racial hierarchies and other ideological preconceptions justified, was partly behind their systematic elimination.

Wells sympathizes with the plight of the poor Tasmanians, but his rhetoric is not completely free of racist pronouncements. For example, he calls their extermination "ruthless" but, at the same time, identifies the victims as members of "inferior races." While impugning the colonists for fifty years of mistreatment, he wonders why "the human likeness" of the Tasmanians did not elicit sympathy (or guilt) from the colonists. Here, too, one detects the unilinear bias in the phrase "human likeness," for it implies that the Tasmanians resembled, but not necessarily were, human beings and that their similarity to whites should have given the colonists some pause.

In *The Outline of History*, written in 1918–1919 and first published in 1920, Wells reviews the Tasmanian issue, now from a standpoint less distorted by preconceived notions about human groups. Reassessing Tasmanian history more impartially, he poses a twofold question: what accounts for the Tasmanians' primitivity? And how do they relate to civilized man? These questions are integral to the chapter entitled, "The Neanderthal Man, An Extinct Race." Here, he explains that between 15 and 25,000 years before the present (133), the Tasmanians became geographically detached from the human race, their taxonomic kin, and became arrested in their cultural, social, and technological development. Wells then equates their way of life to that of later-Paleolithic mankind, namely to the Neanderthals, basing this assumption on the fact that the Tasmanians had a tool industry resembling material excavated from lower-Paleolithic strata in Western European sites. In closing, Wells makes the cogent distinction that the Tasmanians "were of the same species as ourselves," even though they lived like Neanderthals; unlike the latter, the Tasmanians were *not* a distinct subspecies of the genus *Homo*. To establish their sapient legacy, he traces their descent from early-modern ancestors whose cultural ways had for some time paralleled those of the Neanderthals, only to supersede them by great leaps and bounds. The Tasmanians, then, were genuine *Homo sapiens* whose socio-cultural and technological progress had been arrested early in the Paleolithic Epoch. To explain this phenomenon further, he theorizes that, because they were remote from human competition, they "lagged behind the rest of the human brotherhood" (83). Wells even elevates the Tasmanians above the Cro-Magnons behaviorally (83).

Essentially, as I suggested, there were two ways of looking at the Tasmanians. Cook's entries exemplify one view (if his journal account can be accepted at face value): observant and relatively free of pre-judgments, it efficiently preserves what is experienced. To a degree, Cook is a detached observer whose standpoint adumbrates that of the modern cultural anthropologist. The other perspective is prone to distortion: the explorer encounters native people with preconceived notions about civilization, progress, and inferiority. For this reason mainly, Péron, Broca, and others assumed that the Tasmanians were a *sui generis* people, ignoble savages whose human identity was zoologically uncertain. Classified as inferior beings, the Tasmanians, among others, would consequently have few intrinsic rights and, worse, could be valued as commodities or diversions. In 1863, Reverend Thomas Atkins, for example, descanted on the lowliness of the Tasmanians. Their demise, according to him, was providentially inescapable, for the Bible dictated that the commercial progress of civilization will inevitably supplant "savage tribes who live by hunting and fishing, and on the wild herbs, roots, and fruits of the earth." The Tasmanians, therefore, had only themselves to blame for not complying "with the conditions on which 'the Lord of the whole earth' granted to the first progenitors of our race" (cited in Montagu [1976]:169).

The last of the Tasmanians, William Lanney and Vivienne Trucanini, hoped that their final wish—to be buried in peace—would be respected. But, in 1869, Lanney's corpse was treated as a biological relic. According to one account, the medical establishment was not about to let the last of the Tasmanians escape the lab and the museum:

> In the morgue the body was viciously mutilated: the head, hands and feet removed and only the torso and limbs were left to bury. However, on the same night as the interment, two groups planned to exhume even these remains. Discovering their rivals had beaten them to the body, the leader of the group

smashed down the door to the morgue where the remains had been removed, only to discover 'a few particles of flesh' remained [Urry 11–13; quoted by Rudgley 3].

The chief house surgeon of the Colonial Hospital and a distinguished member of the Royal Society of Tasmania, a Dr. Stockwell, made a tobacco pouch out of Lanney's skin; the head was never found. Trucanini died in 1876, was interred, but then exhumed, to be displayed in the museum of the Royal Society of Tasmania (Rudgley 4).

It would be profoundly ironic if one were to read "The Day Is Done" in connection with the paleoanthropological research of the 1930s. To do so would reveal the prevailing opinion that the Neanderthals evolved into early-modern man. If the story is read in that sense, the demise of Hwoogh, as an instance of parricide, becomes more meaningful: what the Cro-Magnons do not understand is that in rejecting Hwoogh, their genetic forebear, they are disowning their own heritage. Ironically, he is never wholly purged from their lives, for his genes persist in them. Nevertheless, as the children ransack Hwoogh's cave, it is clear that they are desecrating their own past. Had Del Rey written with greater scientific accuracy, "The Day Is Done" would have been a more evocative and ironic work of fiction.

7

William Golding's
The Inheritors:
The Great Divide

In *The Inheritors*, William Golding uses a passage from *The Outline of History* (I.88) epigraphically to criticize H. G. Wells's April 1921 depiction of the Neanderthals as prototypical ogres. His explicit intention is "to overthrow" the anthropological content of "The Grisly Folk" (Oldsey & Weintraub 49–50). Ironically, Golding's Neanderthal image, although true to received authority in 1955, fails to rehabilitate Wells's persona: the latter is merely re-cast invalidly in Boulesque and phrenological terms.

Objecting to Wells's portrayal of Neanderthal as a monster and of early-modern humans as heroic pioneers, Golding reverses their roles, making the Neanderthal a benign creature and our direct human ancestors brutal savages. As Patrick Reilly observes, "*The Inheritors* stands Wells on his head by depicting the Neanderthals as gentle and innocent, the newcomers as vicious and aggressive" (170). Golding's greatest innovation in the novel is to bring his readers into intimate contact with archaic beings by viewing the later-Paleolithic world through the eyes of a typical Neanderthal: his youthful protagonist, Lok. Several scholars extol Golding's effort. James Baker believes that Golding successfully re-creates the Neanderthal's "naive level of perception" (23). Peter S. Alterman thinks that the acute sensuous perception and "telepathy" Golding attributes to his Neanderthals highlight an important theme: that of the alien in science fiction. In contrast to modern humans, the Neanderthal aliens are innocent and moral beings whose presence defines for the reader "what is human and what is not" (3, 11).

However, not all agree that the Neanderthal mentality in the novel is a realistic advantage. As Philip Redpath explains, cognitive disabilities leave the Neanderthals vulnerable to danger; thus, in their minds, since "there is no bridge between words and what they mean," they are fatally handicapped (144). He rightly suggests that, "Lok and his kind are destroyed because of their lack of reason" (146). Mark Kinkead-Weekes and Ian Gregor believe that the Neanderthal "sense and instinct" (as Golding renders it) provide for an "abnormally rich life," despite the fact that characters such as Lok cannot think abstractly (67, 73). To be "abnormally" receptive to sense stimuli but deficient in abstract thought, to my mind, may be the right balance for a cheetah pursuing a gazelle, but, for a human being in the Würm glaciation, these qualities are liabilities. I therefore agree with Redpath: Golding's Neanderthals are, for some reason, cognitively deficient. The question I will try to answer is: why did Golding disable this subspecies if, indeed, he wanted to rectify Wells's distortions in "The Grisly Folk"? I propose that Golding's vision of an archaic mentality, mediated by a third-person narrator, is the consequence of errors about the Neanderthals stemming from Marcellin Boules' anatomical misconstruction and from craniometric theory.

Before further considering Golding's depiction of the Neanderthal mind, let me offer background information on how opinions about prehistoric intelligence are gathered from the fossil record. According to Ralph L. Holloway, we learn about prehistoric brain development directly from the study of endocasts—artificial or real fossil crania (98–9). These tell us about brain volume, convolutional details, the meningeal vessels, and other morphological features, including the shape and asymmetries of the cerebral cortex. A complementary method for learning about prehistoric neuroanatomy is to study the brains of living animals comparatively and then to correlate brain anatomy to behavior. And, in the case of archaic man, artifacts such as tools and other materials can also be sources of information about intelligence.

As I mentioned earlier, the cranial fragments of the Neanderthals found in the later nineteenth century perplexed researchers, mainly because they combine archaic and modern features (Stringer [1988]: 368–70). Marcellin Boule arrived at his hypothesis on Neanderthal mental deficiency from dubious presuppositions about the shape of the head and brain and about what these data said about intelligence. Boule postulated that the frontal cortex was the focus of "higher" intelligence: the deficiency he ascribed to the Neanderthal frontal lobe, therefore, led him to conclude that they were mentally defective. In determining intelligence from the shape of the cranium, Boule was practicing craniometry. We are already familiar with this questionable methodology from our discussion of Verne's reference to Camper's angle. What I did not mention previously was that craniometrists presupposed that "higher" mental faculties were in the front of the brain while sensorimotor capacities were in the rear (Gould [1981]:77). Accordingly, the Neanderthal profile—sloping forehead, long skull, bulbous occipital region—was explicit: he was advanced in sensorimotor capacity but inept at higher thought. One large piece of Boule's neat puzzle, however, did not fit: Neanderthal cranial capacity (1600 cubic centimeters on average) was as large as, if not bigger than, that of the average modern human. This created a problem for Boule. The Neanderthal's big brain, according to phrenological thought, meant that had the capacity for abstract thought, but this assumption did not fit Boule's anatomical portrayal of the Neanderthal as a dolt. Perhaps in desperation, he sidestepped the issue of brain volume.

With respect to the Neanderthal, today's anthropologists seem quite reluctant to correlate neuroanatomy with intelligence. Ashley Montagu, in 1968, rejected the idea that the shape of a Neanderthal endocast could tell us anything about his mind. His counter-argument had a firm anatomical foundation: the frontal cortex of this being was quite well developed after all; and the prominent eyebrow ridges were what made the forehead appear to be low. Thus, argued Montagu, the Neanderthal was as intelligent as modern man (67). He was not the only distinguished anthropologist to hold this opinion. David Pilbeam, looking at the fossil artifacts, in 1972, judged the Neanderthal to have been a "fully sapient human being" (180), while Christopher Stringer reservedly stated that the intellectual significance of the shape and size of his brain is currently "unclear" ([1988]:370).

In contrast to these views, we can cite several that revive Boule's theory. H. Chandler Elliott, in 1969, believing that the Neanderthal's frontal lobe was indeed smaller than that of early-modern humans, maintained that his large occipital region endowed him with "larger areas to judge sensation" (218). The distinguishing feature of this human being's mind was a capacity for "subtle sense analysis," giving him an advantage over early-modern humans in the area of sensory discrimination (Elliott 219). In 1981 Robert Jastrow, an astronomer, opined that the Neanderthal was quite intelligent but that the shape of the cranium demonstrated his inferiority to modern man in the creative realms of music, of art, and of science. This inferiority also meant that he was maladapted to adversity (140–1).

Despite the belief of Leakey and Lewin that tools are not reliable indicators of brain power ([1977]:183), such artifacts, I think, provide some degree of comparative insight into the mentality of the prehistoric manufacturer. Fundamentally, phrenological theories of Neanderthal intelligence, postulating deficient higher faculties (low forehead) and heightened sensory capacity (large occiput), were incongruent with Neanderthal achievements, namely with his stone-tool traditions, skilled hunting practices, social structure, ritualism, and ability to survive during the Würm glaciation. The standpoint of Montagu, of Pilbeam, and (to some degree) of Stringer, then, would appear defensible. This brings me to the pivotal question: where does Golding's Neanderthal stand?

Directly correlating neuroanatomy to intelligence, Golding imagines a brain dysfunction for his Neanderthal population. For this reason, the Neanderthals of *The Inheritors* seem to have stumbled directly out of Boule's laboratory. Golding emphasizes the perceptual experience of Lok (textually mediated through a third-person narrator) from the inside out. To understand what this means from an evolutionary standpoint, I need to digress briefly on the subject of sensory physiology. J. L. Rappaport, in 1971, formulated a model for understanding the perceptual process (Kerr 131–4) that will assist us in mapping Lok's interior experience. To begin with, sensory receptors in the eye, ear, nose, and tongue receive external stimuli which are transformed into nerve impulses. These impulses, in turn, are conveyed (or *transduced*) to the brain along a specific neurological path: the eyes and ears, for example, connect with the brain through the optic and acoustic cranial nerves which, in turn, connect with the visual and auditory cortex. Within a sensory modality such as seeing or hearing, the nerve impulses, as pieces of information, are labeled and organized into larger constructs called *precepts*. At a third level, these constructs are further organized into mental images or *concepts*. And finally, *cognition* or knowing occurs: organized information then has meaning for the individual.

The most characteristic aspect of Lok's consciousness, and one incommensurate with the cultural and technological achievements of the Neanderthal, is (in Rappaport's terminology) an interruption of nerve-impulse *transduction* to the brain. Lok, it seems, is unable to process what he senses. In one scene, he spies a band of early-modern humans who, having kidnapped Neanderthal children, are decamping. To Lok, their frenetic activity is meaningless. He hears the noises and labels what he senses in the aggregate as a "laugh-sound"; the auditory stimuli, in turn, "make a picture in his head" (104–5). But beyond the *preceptual* level, Lok's thinking cannot progress: what the early-modern humans are doing and how it affects the lost children is incomprehensible to him. Because his interpretative skills are stunted, he can only connect the "laugh-sound" to an irrelevant analogue, removed in time and space from the emergency unfolding before him. The "laugh-sound," rather than denoting the imminent embarkation of the early-modern humans, is described merely as "tangled like weed on the beach after a storm" (104). Figurative virtuosity notwithstanding, this phrase is only tangentially meaningful, being causatively unrelated to the "laugh-sound" and to the phenomenal reality from which it originates. When the child Liku screams as she is placed in one of the boats, a second mental artifact surfaces. This time, her shrieking, instead of being identified as a child's cry, is associated with an alarming primal memory: the sound of a horse being torn apart by a saber-toothed tiger. The *precept* of primal terror which Liku communicates does not literally register in Lok's mind where a great divide exists between the sensory and cognitive faculties. The brain dysfunction that Golding inflicts upon the classic Neanderthal, however, has no scientific basis, belonging as it does to the annals of phrenology.

Lok's internal and external awareness, instead of being two aspects of a unified consciousness, operate independently. "Outside" Lok is the sensory receiver; the phrase "outside of Lok" refers, precisely, to his awareness of the exterior environment (124). At the same time, "inside" refers to the interior or mental consciousness. Lok understandably prefers the "outside" to the "inside" consciousness because the former relates him to the world, spatially and temporally, whereas the "inside" is a turbulent zone in which the mind's eye helplessly surveys disconnected mental images. It is no surprise to hear that Outside-Lok is on the alert for approaching danger in the scene just described (154). But Lok's thoughts cannot be trusted to represent reality accurately. Seeming to suffer from multiple-personality disorder, he hears disembodied voices that tell him what to do. In effect, Golding's Neanderthal suffers, at once, from sensory overload and cognitive deprivation. Lok can neither react nor adapt to the challenges of the environment.

Golding's description of Neanderthal mentality raises a cogent question. Instead of imagining a human group capable of surviving during a glaciation, of formulating ritual and a rudimentary belief in the after-life, or of developing a tool technology, he presents a fragmented mind, the nature of which is extrapolated incorrectly from endocasts. His Neanderthal, therefore, seems to have more in common with Boule's fictive imbecile than with the fossil record that Wells appreciated in 1899 and would reappraise in 1929.

So why did Golding create a Boulesque Neanderthal? One possibility is that the stereotype balances two fictive imperatives: the re-humanization of Wells's anthropoidal man; and the subordination of this predecessor to the early-moderns who inherited the human estate 24,500 years ago. A second possibility accounting for the stereotype is that Golding accepted it as a valid depiction of Neanderthal consciousness: he might have been scientifically conservative. We know that the credibility of Boule's work peaked in 1955 (the year of *The Inheritors'* publication), but that, in 1957, his ideas would be discredited. I would like to explore both these possibilities briefly.

In the first place, Golding's phrenologically derived Neanderthal might reflect his ambivalence towards quantitative science, specifically for its putative inhibition of the human imagination. A 1965 essay, "Egypt from My Inside," helps to illuminate *The Inheritors*. Golding writes about his youthful fascination with dynastic Egypt which was not grounded in archaeology but in intuitive and humanistic ideas transcending the work of retrieval, of classification, and of reconstruction. For the young Golding, Egypt was a fecund culture to which he related intuitively (71). Distinguishing between this intuitive appreciation of Egypt and the matter of "exact scholarship or painstaking science," the cumulative stores of which confound its "mystery," Golding cites Herodotus as the forerunner of the modern Egyptologist. Having studied the skulls of dead Persian and Egyptian soldiers comparatively (*The Histories* III.13:[207]), Herodotus recounts the hearsay opinion that the thickness of Egyptian skulls in contrast to the more fragile Persian ones can be ascribed to the former's exposure to the sun; the latter's thinness resulted from the habit of wearing "skull-caps." This dubious conclusion, in Golding's view, represents an intellectual opposition in the Western mind between the analytical and intuitive faculties—between "common sense and experiment," on the one hand, and "vivid imagination and intellectual sloth" on the other (72). Golding's ambivalence towards "the Herodotean method" denies neither its efficiency nor its potency. But he disdains the strict analysis of human history responsible for "the lame giant of civilization." The quantitative mentality, Golding argues, cannot distinguish between a puzzle and a mystery—that is, between a question or contrivance designed to test ingenuity and a profound, inexplicable quality or character. But Golding also acknowledges that, to some extent, the Egyptians despoiled their own ethos, reducing the mystery of their "high art" and eschatology to "daylight banality" (73). The self-advertisement and opulence of the pharaohs, he observes, occluded their spirituality (73).

Golding believes that the ineffable humanity of ancient Egypt, resonating from its artifacts, transcends "the dull method of statistical investigation" (81). Without repudiating the importance of science as a means of learning about antiquity, the author identifies himself as "an Ancient

Egyptian" on the grounds that he, too, is unreasonable, spiritually pragmatic, and inclines to "ambiguous belief" (82). If *The Inheritors* also expresses this attitude, then the presence of a Boulesque stereotype is immaterial since Golding is more concerned with satisfying the imaginative priorities of his fiction. Conforming to the most plausible theory about Neanderthal mentality would have been irrelevant to the primary task: the removal of Wells's distortions—for which Golding substitutes his own.

In the second place, Golding's use of the stereotype may reflect a scientific conservatism inasmuch as Boule's model was legitimate as late as 1955. The anatomists, William Strauss and A. J. E. Cave, proved conclusively, in 1957, that the La Chapelle-aux-Saints Neanderthal which Boule had thought representative of the subspecies was, in fact, arthritically deformed (an ironic twist on Virchow's theory) and therefore atypical (Campbell 306). As we recall, Boule took these skeletal features (a slouch, along with simian-like jaws, vertebrae, and pelvis) as evidence of primitivity. The Strauss and Cave study suggested, conversely, that the Neanderthal was quite human and might have been an ancestor or close relative after all.

Golding's Boulesque Neanderthal is either a literary critique of statistical investigation or, conversely, a conformity with science. In either case, *The Inheritors* is consistent with a prominent, long-standing school of anthropological thought, but one that was about to become outmoded.

8

Arthur C. Clarke's
2001: A Space Odyssey:
"the promise of humanity"

In *Civilization and Its Discontents* (1929), Sigmund Freud (1856–1939), the Austrian neurologist and founder of psychoanalysis, approaches the phenomenon of human aggression psychologically, philosophically, and historically, and his commentary finds its way, in one form or another, into many discussions of those who believe that man is inherently aggressive. What he calls "the inclination to aggression" can be detected within ourselves as a universal trait and can justifiably be assumed to exist in others (69). Whereas the validity of this generalization is arguable, Freud's belief that the aggressive impulse disturbs human relations appears self-evident. Because of "this primary mutual hostility of human beings," an impulse inherent in the human personality, an ordered society has to work incessantly to avoid internal discord. Rational man cannot channel this destructive power for good, for "instinctual passions" are stronger (69). One example of the futility of the civilized effort in the control of aggression is capital punishment. Paradoxically, civilization prosecutes criminals in order to prevent "the crudest excesses of brutal violence" (70).

It is not that people are in the grip of a destructive passion working against their better judgment or thwarting their will, for even a conscientious person finds it difficult, perhaps even undesirable, "to give up the satisfaction of the inclination to aggression" (81). Aggression, according to Freud, is more an effect of man's self-defensiveness than of his acquisitiveness. The aggressive proclivity allows one to identify and repel attackers. It brings a sense of wariness and security, and for this reason human beings "do not feel comfortable without it" (72). As an "original, self-subsisting instinctual disposition," the aggression impulse appears to have originated at the very beginning of human consciousness. The insoluble problem is that this inclination is, at once, a wellspring of survival yet "the greatest impediment to civilization" (81).

Freud's aggression phenomenon reputedly emanates from two contending forces at the core of human society. On the one hand, the civilizing process, which unifies individuals, families, races, and nations (81), serves Eros. Against this force is the natural, aggressive instinct, which is primordial, self-centered, and libidinous. In Freud's scheme, the aggressive instinct emanates from the mind and is "the main representative of the death instinct," a drive that shares "world-dominion" with Eros. It is precisely this antithetical struggle in history, "between the instinct of life and the instinct of destruction," that constitutes the drama of the human species. Freud portrays "the struggle for life of the human species" in terms of the dialectical conflict between Eros and Thanatos (82).

While Freud provides a psychological context and explanation for the aggressive instinct, Raymond Dart establishes what many believe is a persuasive zoological correlative to Freud's thesis that aggression is an innate, primordial force and a perennial threat to human relations on all levels. Dart infers the principles of his thesis from faunal and artifactual remains found at a South African stratified cave site near Makapansgat (northern Transvaal Province), the main materials of which are dated to be between 2.6 and 3.0 million years old (Grine 329–30). According to Fred E. Grine, the site originally was mined for limestone between 1925 and 1935. It was during this interval that fossils were discovered. In 1947, J. W. Kitching found the first hominid specimen that Dart described in 1949 and named *Australopithecus prometheus*. Kitching and his co-worker, A. R. Hughes, later retrieved dozens of specimens from the limework rubble, all of which have been associated with *Australopithecus africanus* (Dart's coinage meaning "southern ape"). This nomenclature referred to a juvenile hominid specimen he had found in 1925, at a place called Taung (South Africa) (Dart [1925]:140–8). The specimen uniquely exhibits both anthropoidal and human features, respectively: a small brain and large snout but upright posture, bipedalism, and human-like dentition. With a large amount of fossil material at Makapansgat to work with, Dart wished to learn about the behavior and culture of *Australopithecus*. He determined that the copious faunal assemblages, containing bone (osteo-), tooth (donto-), and horn (keratic), evidenced, for the *Australopithecines*, a prehistoric technology and culture. He fashioned the Greek neologism, osteodontokeratic, to describe this bone-tooth-horn culture, and he published his theory in 1957.

In his book *Adventures with the Missing Link* (1959), Dart sums up his findings. The *Australopithecines* belong to the genus *Homo*. On the basis of their tool use, and despite a small brain size, these creatures are indisputably direct ancestors of modern man. Furthermore, "their sapient human posterity" is responsible for their tool culture. This seems to prove that they are the founders of human culture inasmuch as they devised "the saws, scrapers, axes, poniards and digging tools that served mankind until very recent times" (183).

Along with this reputed technological achievement, *Australopithecus* has an unpleasant side, according to a hypothesis Dart published in an article entitled, "The Predatory Transition from Ape to Man" (1954). For Dart, some forty-two fractured baboon skulls, along with other specimens, provided sound forensic evidence to support the claim that *Australopithecus* was a carnivore that hunted animals and that "ruthlessly killed fellow australopithecines" (183). Not only was he a bold hunter and murderer, but this creature was also a cannibal (191). As the cave breccias revealed, *Australopithecus* protected his meat from "other carnivorous marauders" (191). From this collection of material, Dart infers that the preying upon big animals, such as those at Makapansgat, was a typically human habit (199). In addition, all prehistoric men, in common with primitive modern human beings, were hunters and flesh eaters (199). This led Dart to the boldly provocative statement that, "we are all at heart killers" (199).

The theory of aggressive *Australopithecines* establishes erect bipedalism as a genetic heritage for the genus *Homo*. Dart reasoned that only in the standing position could *Australopithecus* have wielded a club and hurled stones while in the process of attacking and killing prey. His success as a hunter, therefore, was directly contingent on his posture. Without the persistent use of osteodontokeratic tools, the erect posture in these "protomen" would be inconceivable; and since he lacked fangs, he was incapable of hunting without these implements (203).

Another influential aggressionist to enter the scene in the 1960s was Robert Ardrey, an eloquent and prolific writer on natural science. The author of such well-known books as *African Genesis* (1961), *The Territorial Imperative* (1966), and *The Hunting Hypothesis* (1976), Ardrey knew Dart personally and stridently advocated the latter's theory of aggression. In *African Genesis*, Ardrey recapitulates Dart's most telling conclusions. It is specifically because man was a killer that he emerged from the anthropoid line and prospered (29). Dart's evolutionary hypothesis, according to Ardrey, is that "a line of killer apes" diverged from the non-aggressive primate background. "We" (that is, *Homo sapiens sapiens*) learned to stand erect as a necessity of hunting life because we no longer had fangs, teeth, or claws. In the beginning, the "margin of survival" became a rock, a stick, and a heavy bone. Hand-held weapons had a morphological effect: "the use of the weapon meant new and multiplying demands on the nervous system for the co-ordination of muscle and touch and sight" (29). Consequently, an enlarged brain developed in modern man (29). It is therefore incorrect to assume that man created the weapon. For Dart (according to Ardrey), the reverse was true: it is the weapon that fathered the man. Only in this way did archaic man, endowed with a big brain and stone axes, destroy his predecessors who, like *Australopithecus*, fought only with bones. All of human history hinges on this presumed reality: superior weapons make the difference in human evolution (31). Ardrey concludes that, if the weapon is part of our animal legacy (as Makapansgat suggests), then our devotion to it is instinctive (199).

The ethologist Konrad Lorenz, in *On Aggression* (1963), re-states Dart's thesis that aggression is instinctual. Under natural conditions, aggressiveness actually helps to ensure the survival of the individual and of the species. Because Lorenz thought that aggression was "an essential part of the life-preserving organization of instincts" (48), he concurred with Raymond Dart, an indebtedness this passage explicitly reflects: "An unprejudiced observer from another planet, looking upon man as he is today, in his hand the atom bomb, the product of his intelligence, in his heart the aggression drive inherited from his anthropoid ancestors, which this same intelligence cannot control, would not prophesy long life for the species" (49).

Clarke's fiction resolves the paradox with which Lorenz was grappling. The image of an external observer surveying mankind's inexorable decline into nuclear disaster is reminiscent of a scene in *2001: A Space Odyssey* in which the astronaut, Bowman, having been transfigured into an eternal intelligence after his Star-Gate odyssey, can intervene in human history through fiat in order to prevent a nuclear war. Thus, "He put forth his will, and the encircling megatons flowered in a silent detonation that brought a brief, false dawn to half the sleeping globe" (236). Lorenz's point (which would be Clarke's as well) is that innate aggressiveness, an irrepressible impulse, directs the intelligence to create weapons of mass destruction. An instinct to destruction, therefore, impels human behavior. Paradoxically, in the modern world, the biological mandate to preserve the species actually germinates conditions threatening mankind with extinction (Lorenz 49).

The zoologist Desmond Morris, whose opinion is especially cogent to this debate, describes his purpose in *The Naked Ape* (November 1966) as an attempt "to elevate" the human species to the level of his favorite "animal forms," namely the foxes, crows, and lizards that he enjoyed studying and breeding as a child (iii-ix). This sentiment evokes the central theme of *The Island of Doctor Moreau*. In his effort to strip mankind bare of his pretenses and to reveal him for what he is ("a remarkable, ingenious, brilliant animal" [iv]), Morris outlines an evolutionary history of the human species (one congruent with Dart's) that endorses the killer-ape concept. But the identity of this hominid sub-species, the bearer of this so-called instinct, is not clearly disclosed in Morris' book. I say this because Morris seems to have conflated Dart's killer *Australopithecus* with the later and more evolved *erectus* whose substantive archaeological record of social organization, of sophisticated tool-making, and of co-operation he appropriates, proleptically, to fit Dart's thesis. In effect, Morris's error reiterates Dart's theory not in terms of the Makapansgat fossils, but rather in terms of *erectus*, a later, more humanoid creature. In so doing, Morris (like Clarke) creates a fictional variant of Dart's theory while departing from the fossil record entirely.

Morris's account of human evolution begins with diet. Man's need for animal protein was an evolutionary stimulus. One million years ago, a series of concurrently "shattering" developments transpired in the natural history of the human species. At the center of these dramatic developments were our "ancestral ground-apes" which he differentiates from more primitive arboreal primates. But exactly to what kind of terrestrial proto-man was Morris referring? Since this hominid lived one million years ago, and since it reputedly had a large and anatomically sophisticated brain, it is clearly not *Australopithecus*, for the latter lived over 2.0 million years ago and possessed an ape-like brain volume, ranging in size from 410 to 500 milliliters. Nor is the Neanderthal a likely candidate for Morris's hominid. For although their endocranial volume (1305 to 1614 milliliters) and brain complexity are equivalent to those of modern man and qualify as being "large and high quality," the best-known specimens of this subspecies lived from the period ca. 70,000–50,000 years ago in western Asia and 70,000–35,000 years ago in Europe, not one million years ago (Stringer [1988]:371; Holloway 100). Purporting nonetheless to talk about human "Origins" and about the very first proto-humans, Morris claims the hominids in question had "good eyes" and "efficient grasping hands" and, by virtue of their membership in the primate order, "some degree of social organization" (21).

Even though Morris's primate has little in common with early humans, the author tacitly endorses Dart's thesis: the former assumes that the drive for animal protein pressured this non-descript hominid to "increase [its] prey-killing prowess" (21). For this reason, "vital changes began to take place": an upright, bipedal gait permitted swift pursuit of game; its hands, freed from locomotion, developed into "strong, efficient weapon-holders"; concomitantly, their brains evolved more complex neuro-circuitry, rendering them "brighter, quicker decision-makers." All of these elements "blossomed together" and urged each other on, leading Morris to the Dartist conclusion that "A hunting ape, a killer ape, was in the making" (21).

Morris reveals his indebtedness to Dart and to the osteodontokeratic hypothesis when he states that this hominid moved from being a tool user to being a tool maker. His nebulous subspecies reputedly used natural weapons (that is, faunal bones, mandibles, and horns) before making stone tools. This claim, however, is incorrect on several counts. First, it is *Homo habilis* and not *Australopithecus* that many regard as the first tool maker. Moreover, *erectus*, whose direct ancestor is *habilis*, probably developed the Acheulian industry, a stone-tool technology, from 1.5 million to 200,000 years ago. The Acheulian is characterized by hand axes far more sophisticated than the core-flake tool kits typical of the Oldowan industry (associated with its predecessors in Africa) (Potts 3–5). As of yet no evidence (according to one reputable view) points to the *Australopithecines'* having had any tool industry at all, for "no identifiable stone artifacts have been found in the cave breccias that contain A. africanus remains" (Grine 80). It is certainly true that Eugène Dubois named the Java man *Pithecanthropus erectus* or "upright ape-man." But, ever since that great discovery in 1891, paleoanthropologists have come to agree that this hominid is actually an extinct human form originating in Africa nearly two million years ago. And *erectus* is assuredly no "ground ape." While the first tool user is a genuine member of the genus *Homo*, the hunting and territorial ape is the product of Raymond Dart's misconceptions and of Robert Ardrey's imagination. Following Dart and Ardrey, Morris arrives at the conclusion that "we have arisen essentially as primate predators" (23). His conflation of hominid forms (which is reminiscent of Burroughs' pseudo-anthropology) portrays early man as arguably a more efficient killer than "the old-time carnivores" (19) and as the prototype of the modern murderer.

Anthony Storr's much-acclaimed *Human Aggression* (1968) (which is dedicated to Konrad Lorenz) fuses the psychological and ethical viewpoints of the most prominent aggressionists. He reprises Freud's thesis when he calls man an unparalleled savage, "the cruellest and most ruthless species that has ever walked the earth" (x). And he echoes Freud's assumption that we are fully aware of our murderous tendencies: "we know in our hearts that each one of us harbors within himself those same savage impulses which lead to murder, to torture and to war" (x). Storr's thinking is explicitly Freudian: each person reflects on this indwelling, aggressive penchant which is essential to survival but in need of conscientious repression. The ethological aspect of Storr's thesis, influenced no doubt by Lorenz, is that an aggressive character is needed defensively against predators; furthermore, it is both "the basis of intellectual achievement" and "of the attainment of independence" (x). Man's aggressive proclivity allows him to direct his life and to influence his environment. As a result, this large endowment of aggressiveness guarantees his survival (xii). The difference between Freud and Storr on the control of aggressiveness is that the former envisages its intra-psychic suppression and conversion from a harmful to a constructive or neutral drive whereas the latter emphasizes its evolutionary function: the preservation both of the individual and of the species (xiii).

Dart's theory of the killer ape as a direct human ancestor received a serious blow when C. K. Brain, a geologist and director of the Transvaal Museum, challenged the contention that *Australopithecus* killed baboons (and his own kind) with long bones. The skull holes that Dart maintained were the result of clubbings Brain attributes to leopard teeth. To refute Dart's theory, Brain calculated the distance between holes and then compared these data to the dentition of modern predators. The distance between the lower canines of the African leopard matched the punctures in the baboon skulls (Johanson & Edey 66). Brain proceeded to outline a hypothetical scenario: leopards killed both baboons and *Australopithecines*, devouring the carcasses in trees. The remains fell to the ground and, over thousands of years, washed down into dolomitic-limestone fissures and then farther down into the sink-holes created by large trees. This could explain why these bones were found together. Rather than being the garbage dump of carnivorous hominids, Brain and others point out, the site really was the refuse heap of leopards.

A comparative aspect of Brain's work also undermines Dart's predation thesis. Brain studied a contemporary tribe to learn how human beings and contemporaneous fauna interacted with one another. Several thousand goat remains dumped outside of a Khoikoi village were regularly scavenged by dogs. The dog-eaten remains, Brain determined, resembled the bones of animals found at Makapansgat. The condition of the faunal remains at Makapansgat could therefore be ascribed to hominid predation, but more so to prowling scavengers, for the resemblance between the fossils and the extant bones suggested that hyenas rather than *Australopithecines* were responsible for the many bones found in the cave breccias. In his paper, "The Transvaal Ape-Man-Bearing Cave Deposits," Brain does not rule out the possibility that hominids were responsible for the devoured fauna at Makapansgat (which would also mean cannibalism). But he strongly suggests that Dart's conclusions about osteodontokeratic culture and about *Australopithecus prometheus* (the species discovered at Makapansgat) are incorrect. Anthropologists have since pointed out that the leopard, not the hyena, was probably responsible for the Makapansgat specimens inasmuch as the hyena, as a scavenger, does not store bones (Johanson & Edey 68).

Brain's findings encouraged Ashley Montagu, an anthropologist, to formulate a counter-theory. Montagu, who wrote extensively on the subject of human violence, in 1968 categorically rejected the idea that man is innately aggressive and instinctively territorial (122). Man, he affirms, is not instinctual at all. Since instincts are statically encoded behavior, new challenges of the environment such as those facing human ancestors required "thought-out problem-solving responses" rather than automatic reactions. On this basis, he concludes that most human beings are not born with instinctive drives such as aggression and have no predisposition to injure others. Instead, man behaves aggressively "from the models of aggression that condition him in a particular environment" (122). Nor is territoriality an "instinctive" predisposition (122). Montagu points out that, while some societies are territorially minded, others are not; so it is not a universal behavioral trait. People learn to feel and think about territory in a certain way, and they are not born with invariable tendencies in this regard (122).

In a 1976 monograph on human aggression, Montagu explains that the terrible cruelties committed by a few people should not indict the human species (301). Instances of non-aggressive people demonstrate that cruelty and destruction are not universal traits, and he rejects as unsound the claim "that man is an innate killer" (304). Those who argue to the contrary, he observes, rely on incorrect extrapolations from animal to man, on one-sided arguments, on the misinterpretation of facts as they relate to humans, and on irrelevant anecdotes (306). The longevity of the human species depends, in his view, not on how well man kills his fellow man but on ingenuity and co-operation, without which society is doomed to extinction (307). In dismissing the notion of human instinct, Montagu does not deny that there is a genetic component to human behavior; to a degree, behavior is always the expression of an interaction between "genetic tendencies" and "environmental influences" (309). Unlike animals, humans have a plastic nature: culture influences genetic constitution. Thus, human behavior is not deterministic even though genetic factors play a role in the way people act. "The conditioning environment," Montagu relates, "interacts with the genetic potentials and the resulting behavior is the expression of that interaction" (309). Nor should one believe that cultures are genetically determined: they differ from one another in terms of "the history of their experiences" (309). For those who insist that there exists a primitive region of the brain where aggressive impulses originate, Montagu offers some clarification. The "appropriate experience" can readily organize areas of the brain and certain genes "to produce aggressive behavior." But that is not equivalent to saying that there is a center or region of the brain responsible for violence or that there are genes making aggression inevitable (314). Those who maintain that the human race is a "scarred species, branded with the mark of Cain, [and] driven by archaic impulses to violence and destruction" (315) are deceived. Though an intriguing thought, it is groundless (319).

To the paleoanthropologists Richard E. Leakey and Roger Lewin (1977), the idea of human descent from a homicidal cannibal is a "dangerous fiction" (8–9). Like Montagu, they contend that the turning point in human evolutionary history is not early man's impulse to kill and eat his own kind but the inclination to share with one another. The act of sharing, in their view, transformed a social ape-like creature into a cultural one who could live in a structured and organized society (8–9). Early man must, therefore, have shared both jobs and food. Admittedly, meat-eating helped to propel our ancestors along the way to socialization, but this was only one aspect of a number of related "socially-oriented changes" involving plant gathering and the sharing of goods (8–9). Their interesting riposte to Dart, Ardrey, and Lorenz, is that hunter-gatherer societies such as those of the *Australopithecines* were part of the natural order and actually the least prone to aggression. Sedentary farming communities, on the other hand, had more of a reason to fight in order to protect coveted possessions. The underlying cause of human conflict, especially in the modern world, is the need to protect what one owns (10). As Montagu explains, environmentally dictated experience, as in the case of the early farmer, promoted violence. That "mankind is incorrigibly belligerent" and that "war and violence are in our genes," however, are ideas constituting a dangerous modern myth (192–3). A basic understanding of evolutionary biology discounts aggressionism inasmuch as the penchant for killing one's own kind, especially when a population is limited in number (as was the case for the *Australopithecines*), is disadvantageous and would promote extinction. The success of a species depends on having large numbers of descendants which enhances adaptability. If homicide was the norm, the human species would have wiped itself out millions of years ago (197). Moreover, the aggressionists fail to consider the analogical evidence fully: aggression is not a universal instinct in the animal kingdom (199). Neither Leakey nor Lewin deny that we live in a dangerous world replete with weapons of mass destruction (232). They optimistically console the reader with the fact that human intelligence can secure "the peaceful and equitable survival of humanity" (243).

Richard Wrangham and Dale Peterson, in their discussion of how primates are portrayed in literature and other media, cite *2001: A Space Odyssey* as a contribution to the 1960s' debate on human intelligence and war, and their opinion provides a way of bridging theory and fiction and an interesting preamble to my reading of the story. A theme of Clarke's fiction, according to Wrangham and Peterson, is that war, as "one of the defining marks of humanity," sets man apart from nature. In my view, Clarke unnecessarily circumvents the evolutionary questions that Dart and others raise. Rather than being a plausible extension of the debate on the evolutionary roots of aggression, Clarke's fiction detours to an extraterrestrial cause. The inclination to warfare, in his imaginative account, is not ingrained in the human character as the by-product of primate evolution; rather, it is an idea "implanted by aliens" (Wrangham and Peterson 22). Consequently, the anthropological content of the story is pre-empted. *2001: A Space Odyssey* contributes nothing substantive to the debate of the 1960s beyond an endorsement of Dart's thesis.

Although Clarke ascribes the origin of human violence to aliens rather than to the complex processes of evolutionary biology, he nevertheless adheres closely to Dart's popular conjectures (perhaps via Ardrey) that are based on his original study of *Australopithecine* fossils. Since Dart's theories, which were eventually disproved, form the scientific substance of *2001: A Space Odyssey*, I will point out precisely how theory is woven into the fiction and how this novel meticulously imitates normal science.

The first chapter, "The Road to Extinction," envisions the man-apes of the African veldt in a period of decline. The creatures Clarke carefully describes resemble *Australopithecus africanus*. The protagonist, Moon-Watcher, an alpha male, stands upright, weighs approximately one hundred pounds, and is a "giant" at five foot five (4). All of these dimensions correspond to those of the gracile form of *Australopithecus* that Raymond Dart discovered. Although Moon-Watcher's body is ape-like, hairy, and muscular, his cranial structure is more human than anthropoid: the forehead is low, and there are ridges over his eye sockets, both of which are primitive traits; but the ubiquitous speaker assures us that he holds "the promise of humanity" in his genes (4). Gazing out over the Pleistocene savanna, Moon-Watcher exhibits the first intimations of intelligence. But his capacity for reflection is definitely limited; in fact, his consciousness is circumscribed in the present moment. That he is in the process of thoughtlessly disposing of his father's corpse for the hyenas to scavenge dramatizes the limits of his intelligence and his sense of isolation from others of his kind.

Moon-Watcher and his kind are foragers, subsisting on a paltry diet of berries, roots, leaves, and small animals. His tribe, consisting of fifty individuals, is territorial, so they howl at an encroaching tribe of *Australopithecines* (5). These displays of anger, like those of primates such as the chimpanzee and lowland gorilla, never turn into anything serious, for the males of each tribe only wrestle with one another and make a noisy scene. Since they have neither fangs, claws, nor lethal weapons, the *Australopithecines* resort to snarling and to gesturing, not to overt violence. They are so busy trying to stay alive through foraging and by avoiding predators such as the leopard that neither side can well afford to waste energy in a fruitless conflict. The idea of cooperation between the two tribes, however, is beyond their comprehension.

Their meager diet is not due to a lack of game but to the hominids' inability to hunt and, more so, to realize that a new approach to life is necessary for survival (6). A twenty-five year old, Moon-Watcher is in his twilight years (the mean survival age being thirty-five): "if his luck continued, and he avoided accidents, disease, predators, and starvation, he might survive for as much as another ten years" (7). But because they are maladapted as savanna hunters, lacking natural weapons for hunting and defense, they remain disadvantaged and scattered. As long as they lack sustenance, they are vulnerable to predatory attacks and to disease, and their numbers could dwindle to extinction. The key to survival and to adaptation, the story rightly implies, is a large self-sustaining population that does not have to live on the ecological margins. This is the dilemma of Clarke's *Australopithecines* in their most vulnerable stage of existence: on their survival ostensibly hinges the fate of *Homo sapiens sapiens* (or so it was thought in the 1960s).

The first major turn in the novel occurs when Moon-Watcher and others come upon the alien monolith (10). Fifteen feet high and five feet wide, the "New Rock" entrances the onlookers through a rhythmic drumming sound and through alterations in color and brightness (11). To map physiology, to study reactions, and to evaluate potentials, the aliens examine the proto-human mind. One man-ape, manipulated to test his manual dexterity and the opposability of thumb and forefinger, fails to make a crude knot from a stalk of grass although another succeeds at this task.

Thus, on the planet Earth, "the first crude knot had been tied" (13). Moon-Watcher's turn as a coerced subject is equally eventful. Obeying silent orders in his brain, he throws pebbles at the monolith, testing and improving his hand-eye coordination with each try (13). He is treated like a Pavlovian dog: the alien power invokes "a feeling of indescribable pleasure," an endorphin-like reward for his fourth throw, a near-bull's eye. Each member of the tribe must repeat the task. Those who succeed receive pleasure; but those who fail are punished by spasms of pain (13). In this way, the aliens train and reconfigure the minds and bodies of the hominids.

In Chapter Three, "Academy," the formation of the *Australopithecines* continues but now more selectively. Moon-Watcher is considered an alpha male and, as such, is more likely to procreate in great numbers; his genetic endowment, therefore, is worthy of investment. As a promising subject, he experiences the inquisitive tendrils of the alien influence "creeping down the unused byways of his brain." At this juncture, the aliens induce a mental image that blocks the territorial defense mechanism Clarke presumes to be innate in the hominid mind: thus, "the usual automatic impulse to drive off invaders of his territory had been lulled into quiescence." This impulse suppressed, another occupies the foreground of Moon-Watcher's consciousness. He sees a nuclear family—male, female and two infants—living in abundant simplicity, well fed, healthy, and secure. Moon-Watcher is then made to compare this image of what could be with his own emaciated and solitary state which reflects the condition of his tribe as a whole. He envies the ideal family and is dissatisfied with his present, solitary state. The recurrent image of the four plump man-apes exasperates him, and he reacts to it. The alien intelligence transforming his brain into "new patterns" (17) conditions him. The intention, of course, is to reform more than just Moon-Watcher himself: "If he survived, those patterns would become eternal, for his genes would pass them on to future generations" (17). Scattered across the globe, strategically located monoliths are at work with other *Australopithecines*, slowly and patiently enlightening them and guiding them away from extinction. A single success, avers Clarke, is enough to change "the destiny of the world" (17).

To dislodge the inherited instincts of the past, the alien power moves this *Australopithecus* to the level of a tool user. About to make the critical transition from gatherer to hunter, Moon-Watcher is impelled to seize "a heavy pointed stone about six inches long" that nearly fits his hand. Surprised by the stone's weight, Moon-Watcher has a sense of power and authority. Because a pig instinctively fears neither the *Aus-*

tralopithecines nor the stone hammer, it makes no sudden effort to avoid the death blow. Moon-Watcher's act evokes wonder and admiration from his kind. They join in the pig killing avidly, wielding sticks and stones. Another crucial event occurs at this point when a nursing female decides to lick the gory stone. This solitary act adds animal protein to the *Australopithecine* diet (we recall Morris's argument), whether they fully realize it or not (19).

In no place is Dart's influence more palpably felt than in the chapter entitled, "The Leopard": it dramatizes osteodontokeratic culture explicitly. The tools that the aliens program the hominids to use grant the man-apes biological ascendancy in the world. The hand-held stones multiply the power of a blow. The bone club lengthens the reach and helps the hunter to avoid the fangs and claws of animals. Although these tools provide limitless supplies of food, other tools are needed to dismember animals. The lower jawbone of an antelope with the teeth intact makes a crude but efficient knife or saw. A gazelle's horn functions as an awl or dagger. Finally, the complete jaw of any animal works as a scraping tool. Clarke's speaker sums up the technological achievement of the hominids: "The stone club, the toothed saw, the horn dagger, the bone scraper" are the inventions that the man-apes need to survive on the African savanna because this technology will make them omnivorous, and a rich and balanced diet means survival and longevity. Thus, the alien technology providing early man with "symbols of power"(21) finds its paleoanthropological origin at Makapansgat, South Africa, and is equivalent to Dart's bone-tooth-horn thesis which he believes spurred human evolution on.

The behavior of the fictive hominids changes because they have new confidence in their ability to slay their enemies and to acquire meat. In the course of a single year after the monolith's edifying work, Moon-Watcher and his tribe are reborn. Since they wield this array of tools well and bring down gazelles, antelopes, zebras and other animals which they slaughter and eat raw, the apprentice hunters, now with an abundance of food, have more leisure time for socialization. They do not associate their new way of life with the monolith standing beside the trail near the river, of course, and probably ascribe their new status (if they think about it at all) to their own efforts. No longer preoccupied with acquiring food, they begin to reflect (21).

For the *Australopithecines*, two additional survival issues have yet to be addressed. One is how to counter predators; the other is how to defend against conspecific enemies. Even though they are proficient hunters, they can only consume their prey at the site of the kill before large scavengers and other predators arrive on the scene to drive them off. Coming upon a wounded antelope, Moon-Watcher coordinates a successful attack against it. He visualizes having the carcass in the cave where it can be consumed and where its remains can be stored without fear of scavengers (22–3). The scent of blood, they know, will surely draw the leopard to the cave. But the *Australopithecines* destroy the leopard in collective defense of their cave even though they wield clumsy weapons (24). Consequently, Moon-Watcher, having experienced foresight, "rightly sensed that the whole world had changed and that he was no longer a powerless victim of the forces around him" (25).

As Moon-Watcher and his band boldly approach the Others or the rival tribe, a stunning event supplants ritualized rage. Moon-Watcher bears a stout branch upon which the severed head of the leopard has been impaled. This trophy and symbol of power has a stick jammed into its mouth so that the fangs are displayed. One-Ear, Moon-Watcher's chief rival, stands his ground, out of ignorance or bravado, but the latter promptly clubs him to death with the leopard head. Their leader assassinated, the Others forget One-Ear and presumably unite with the victorious tribe under Moon-Watcher.

According to Clarke's narrative history of man, for more than 100,000 years after the alien intervention, astounding morphological changes take place. The man-apes, no longer dependent upon large teeth, evolve less prognathic faces. As the snouts recede, the massive jaws become "more delicate." The change in dentition and oral anatomy, allowing hominids to make subtler sounds, moves mankind in the direction of articulate speech (though it is at least one million years away). The descendants of the *Australopithecines* who live through the fourth Ice Age have survived extinction transformed. Here, Clarke enunciates an important Dartist doctrine: "The toolmakers had been remade by their own tools" (30). Technology, in other words, stimulates neuro-circuitry. More highly-developed brains manufacture more sophisticated tools which then stimulates further brain and body evolution, and so on. Clarke's speaker puts it this way:

> For in using clubs and flints, their hands developed a dexterity found nowhere else in the animal kingdom, permitting them to make still better tools, which in turn had developed their limbs and brains yet further. It was an accelerating, cumulative process; and at its end was Man [30].

A great victory over Time is attained when man learns to speak, for then knowledge is passed on from generation to generation; thus, man acquires a past, unlike other animals that are imprisoned in the present moment. When man acquires fire, he perfects his tools, gains greater nutrition from his food, and eventually develops metals. Stone gives way to bronze and then to iron. And eventually agricultural settling replaces nomadic hunting as the human norm.

The greatest irony of all is that the more defenseless man becomes the more lethal the weapons he develops. Thus, "the spear, the bow, the gun, and finally the guided missile had given him weapons of infinite range and all but infinite power" (31). The alien intervention ensuring the evolutionary survival of the genus *Homo* does so by teaching man to use and to refine weapons. But, in the twentieth century, the very means of human survival and evolution produce conditions threatening the human race with extinction. Clarke does not, at this point in the story, explain why this happens, but we may infer the answer. The technologically equipped killer-hominid survives as an effective hunter, a killer of non-human predators, and a warrior. The problem is not, of course, that early man subdues a hostile environment and carves out a homestead for himself, which is the shadowy protocol of the alien intelligence. The third effect of human evolution in the Dartist-Clarke scheme is the most problematic of all: the issue of homicide.

The predatory impulse that the aliens engender in Moon-Watcher claims the life of One-Ear. Yet the Scriptural analogue (Genesis 4:1–26) does not closely obtain here: a shepherd does not murder a farmer; nor are they brothers. But they are conspecific, and it is Moon-Watcher who crosses the threshold between aggressive display and homicide. Like the unsuspecting pig, One-Ear cannot anticipate what Moon-Watcher has planned and is about to carry out. Moon-Watcher, a "genius" and heroic chieftain, is also a premeditated murderer. From the standpoint of natural selection, however, his decision to commit murder may be justified in that it removes a threat and promotes tribal solidarity, along with co-operation between the estranged hominids. But his act is a precedent, nonetheless, and the impulse to kill (if we read Dart's theory in Clarke's fiction) is inextricably related to the hunting impulse.

2001: A Space Odyssey is a deft work of imitation. However, it is not inventive; for, in ascribing man's violent proclivity to the work of aliens, Clarke foregoes an imaginative exploration of evolutionary biology. Unlike Wells in *The Time Machine* (as we shall see), in *2001: A Space Odyssey*, the author does not delve into the terrestrial mechanisms, events, and processes that have had a role in the development of human behavior. An otherwise dead-end species, *Homo sapiens sapiens* is teleologically reshaped in alien terms.

9

H. G. Wells's "The Lord of the Dynamos" and Related Works: "a god among the heathen"

Wells's work on the genesis of primitive religion, an aspect of cultural anthropology, integrates theory into the fiction and is indebted to authorities such as Edward Burnett Tylor and James George Frazer. From ca. 1870 to 1920, opinions on the psycho-social foundations of primitive religion were far from monolithic, and Wells approached the corpus critically.

S. G. F. Brandon has shown that this period abounded in interpretative approaches to the religious sensibility of early man (92–9). Thus, Robert R. Marett (1866–1943) answered Edward Burnett Tylor's (1832–1917) animism with animitism; James George Frazer (1854–1941) focused on the idea of sacrifice and its correlation with man's understandings of nature; Andrew Lang (1844–1912) posited the creator-deity as intuitive in the human mind; Wilhelm Schmidt (1868–1954) extolled the primacy of monotheism; Émile Durkheim (1858–1917) investigated the idea of totemism in the non-rational psyche; Sigmund Freud (1856–1939) found the basis of religion in the Oedipus complex; and Rudolph Otto (1869–1937) explored the nature of the religious experience (the idea of the numinous, for example).

Wells's fictional and non-fictional discourse in this discipline complement one another and contribute significantly to the scientific debate on how religion developed in the mind of primitive man. After reviewing what Darwin had to say on the subject, I will connect his commentary to Wells's in *The Outline of History*. I will circle back to show how

94

the fiction of the 1890s, which is rich with religious meaning, foreshadowed much of what Wells would say three decades later.

Wells's ideas on the genesis of religion have much in common with Darwin's views. In *The Descent of Man* (1871, 1874), Darwin discounts the proposition that "man was aboriginally endowed with the ennobling belief in the existence of an Omnipotent God" (96–7). Citing the research of men like Sir John Lubbock (1834–1913), he assumes the contrary to be true: their fieldwork shows that modern "savages" have no inherent idea of "one or more gods." Nor do they have words in their languages "to express such an idea" (97). That the innate idea of God is probably not universal, Darwin adds, is not meant to challenge the idea of God's existence, to which "the highest intellects" have answered affirmatively (97). Nonetheless, mankind tends to spiritualize the world.

The tendency to believe in "unseen or spiritual agencies," Darwin believes, appears to be universal in uncivilized society (97). Savages tend to imagine that natural objects are animated by spiritual or "living essences," and this tendency gives rise to mono- and to polytheism: savages, with their anthropomorphic propensities, naturally attribute to spirits "the same passions, the same love of vengeance or simplest form of justice, and the same affections which they themselves feel" (98). An unfaltering progression, in the Darwinian view, leads from the belief in unseen spirits, to fetishism, to polytheism, and ultimately to monotheism. The last stage, for a mind poorly developed in reasoning power, features "various strange superstitions and customs" (99).

In *The Voyage of the Beagle*, Darwin refrains from attributing a religious sensibility to the Fuegians on the basis of isolated and anecdotal information, namely about their interment of the dead in caves and mountain forests, their wizards or conjuring doctors, and the prevalent belief in the reality of dreams (185). As the nearest approach to a "religious feeling," Darwin cites their taboo against killing ducklings, an act warranting retributive punishment for the wasting of food; retribution would be administered by "avenging agents" that personify natural elements (185). In *The Autobiography* (1887), he reasons that Hindu polytheism or the Buddhist concept of there being "no god" belies the argument for the intuitive sense of an intelligent God "drawn from the deep inward conviction and feelings which are experienced by most persons" (90–1). All that Darwin can reasonably be sure of, however, is the conviction that natural laws are fixed and therefore predictable, and that the variability of organic beings and the action of natural selection are unpredictable and without design (87). His agnosticism rests on these grounds. However, in the 1870s and early 1880s, he retained an intuitive, albeit it a diminishing,

theism—the belief that "a First Cause having an intelligent mind in some
degree analogous to that of man" is responsible for "this immense and
wonderful universe," as well as for the creation of man; and neither appears
to be "the result of blind chance or necessity" (92).

Whereas Darwin's thinking oscillates between agnosticism and something resembling deism, Wells propounds an anthropology of religion in
the prose discourse that is unequivocally atheistic. Divine revelation, in
the Wellsian view, is neither the cause of social cohesion nor the impetus behind the establishment of a worshipful community. The truth of
the matter, he thinks, is different: pastoralism and not the will of God
was the foundation of Neolithic religion (*OH*.I.126). At this point, Wells
recapitulates the authoritative theories to which he is indebted: the deriva-
tion of the sacrament from magic sacrifices (James Frazer); the worship
of the deceased patriarch (Grant Allen, whom he severely criticizes in a
12 February 1898 review [*EW*.40–6]); animism or the ascribing of a soul
to animate and inanimate things (*OH*.I.128) (E. B. Tylor); and impulse
and emotion (especially the libido) as sources of "deep excitement" (A.
E. Crawley).

From Frazer, Allen, and Crawley, important sources for the understanding of the psychological basis of Neolithic religion, Wells learned
that powerful emotions impelled the Neolithic mentality from dissoci-
ated thoughts to religious concepts. In the earliest stages of the religious
sense, when confusion, emotional conflict, fear, the survival impulse, and
appetite determined Neolithic behavior, early-modern man's thinking
tended to be associative and disconnected. Since natural phenomena
seemed capricious, Neolithic man sought ways of controlling these elements, forces, and processes. For an illusion of security, Neolithic man
empowered the magician, priest, and king, all of whom (according to
Wells) were thought to possess the power to control phenomena, to ward
off danger, and to balance society with nature.

The motives giving rise to sacerdotal paternalism are easily understood. For Wells, post–Neolithic man, like his forebears, pursued "a common purpose in relation to which all men may live happily" and hoped
"to create and develop a common consciousness and a common stock of
knowledge which may serve and illuminate that purpose" (*OH*.I.128). The
activities of the magician or shaman were therefore socially indispensable,
for he was invested with extraordinary power over the phenomenal and
invisible worlds.

One prominent, ordering element in Neolithic life was the fear of
an ancient old man who had somehow been elevated into a tribal god
(*OH*.I.129–30), which was a form of apotheosis. However, along with

apotheosis came the "ideas of sacrificial propitiation, mutilation, and magic murder," all traceable, in Wells's mind, to the agricultural cycle in which the birth-death-rebirth motif was embedded and ritually replicated (129-30).

Neolithic religionists, in Wells's opinion, were degenerate murderers, ritualistic killers who thought human sacrifice could somehow ensure the prosperity of the community. For the Reindeer man, in particular, human sacrifice was correlated to the agricultural and seasonal cycles. The sacrifices at seedtime were propitiatory: men, women, and children were systematically murdered whenever the tribe experienced adversity and "thought the gods were athirst" (*OH*.I.130). More tragic, in Wells's view, was the continuation of this dreadful practice into the Bronze Age, an age of warfare and bloodshed. To illustrate this contention, Wells envisions a sacrificial procession three or four millennia ago in the Wiltshire uplands consisting of priests and chiefs in animal regalia. Assembled in a place like Silbury Hill, they prepare for human sacrifice, paradoxically thought to ensure survival of the community so that "the harvests may be good and the tribe increase" (130). This, Wells disdainfully states, is the summit of human intellectual achievement in the fourth millennia.

That prodigious civilizations practiced human sacrifice fascinated Wells. In fact, the civic community, with its greatest architecture, was founded on the altar of "the seed-time blood sacrifice" (*OH*.I.130). The temples of Egypt and of Mesopotamia, for example, housed shrines containing great figures, often half-animal, before which a sacrificial altar stood. Over the Greek and Roman temples, a divinity in human form, either a god or the symbol of one, generally presided. Priests, priestesses, and temple servants comprised a caste, the membership of which was recruited from the general population. The priestly caste conducted the sacrifice to the temple god, particularly at important times or seasons. Since the seed-time sacrifice was still the focus of worship, as it had been in the Neolithic Age, these practices determined how time would be periodized; thus, temple festivals were the means by which one counted days and organized the calendar.

From the elaborate social functions of the temple, as a center of business, a repository of knowledge, and a center for manufacture, resonated powerful emotions, fear and desire being chief among them. And from these impulses and ideas sprang the deities of the earliest temples, which Wells aptly likens to a social "brain," where records and secrets were housed. As a locus of power, advice, and instruction, it attracted citizens as votaries.

The Genesis of Primitive Religion:
1894–1898

"The Lord of the Dynamos," which first appeared in the *Pall Mall Budget* (September 1894), is an imaginative study of religion and of its genesis in the Neolithic mind. Three dynamos in a British power plant captivate Azuma-zi, an aborigine. Ironically, the noisiest and most defective of the three steam-powered electric generators, described as a snorting, panting, and seething animal, impresses him with its mightiness (76). Inadvertently Holroyd, the crass overseer, contributes to the genesis of Azuma-zi's religion. Absorbing bits and pieces of Holroyd's rambling conversations, Azuma-zi comes to believe that the dynamo has supernatural power. He takes Holroyd literally when the latter dares Azuma-zi to find a "heathen idol" to match the machine. Amidst the din, the native hears Holroyd utter: "'Kill a hundred men. Twelve percent. on the ordinary shares ... and that's something like a Gord'" (77). These disconnected comments on the high voltage of the machine, on its financial value to the company (512n.), and on its metaphoric likeness to "a Gord," respectively, confirm for Azuma-zi the intuition that this is indeed a powerful, supernatural embodiment. Explaining in detail how one can be electrocuted, Holroyd provides a practical illustration through a low voltage shock to Azuma-zi, which confirms the machine's extraordinary power.

Azuma-zi's obsession with the machine and with its "smooth" and "rhythmic" operations (that are like "breathing" [77]) leads to personification. Eventually, he crosses an intellectual threshold when addressing the big dynamo or its indwelling power as "Lord." While watching its belts and components, he experiences odd thoughts. The narrator intrudes at this point with a commentary on the native's mental state: "Scientific people tell us that savages give souls to rocks and trees—and a machine is a thousand times more alive than a rock or a tree" (78). But is an animistic process investing natural objects with life subtly at work in the native's mind? Wells tries to answer this question as Azuma-zi's religion gradually develops.

The native gradually becomes a devoted tender of the dynamo, an activity filling the emotional void left by his own gods being far away. His father, the speaker says, worshipped iron pyrite in the form of a meteoric stone likened to Juggernaut, an avatar of the Hindu god Vishnu to which idolizing worshipers offered their very lives (Sherborne 512n.). Dynamo worship, however, is more complex than the adoration of a natural object, for the machine has no phenomenal analogue. Nor is this nascent religion akin to *Dynamism*, a form or stage of primitive religion referring to "the presence of a power that is ... somehow homogeneous, [but] not yet differentiated as it is in the stage of animism" (Bolle 296–97); by definition, "Dynamism" involves the pre-animistic apprehension of an immanent, diffusive force. What Azuma-zi has before him is a man-made object that is part and parcel of its indwelling deity. The speaker confirms this description, identifying the locus of the native's religious sensibility as the "Dynamo Fetich" (80). This is a significant declaration. The word *fetish* derives from the Portuguese word *feitiço* ("that which is made in order to make" [Lima 314]). Sixteenth-century Portuguese explorers applied the word to cultic figurines they found on the west coast of Africa (Lima 316). The figurine is believed to have embodied supernatural energy that could be phenomenally invoked.

The psychological development of fetish religion, as the speaker recounts, moves from a vague sense of presence, to more distinct feelings, to deliberation, and finally to activity on behalf of, or in reaction to, the spiritual entity. Initially, Azuma-zi's active devotion takes the form of bowing before the electric idol or to its indwelling power. He then offers his stewardship to the machine and to its emanative force. At this juncture, adulation and awe become supplication. As a persecuted member of this cult, Azuma-zi expects to have his prayers answered: thus, he petitions the deity to destroy Holroyd whom he considers his tormentor. Coincidentally, as he voices this supplication to the electric god, a gleam of light breaking through the archway is construed as a sign that his service is acceptable (79). Confiding in the dynamo with each maltreatment at Holroyd's hands, he imagines the machine's tonal modulations to be responses to his supplications.

Azuma-zi believes the deity will avenge itself against the persecutor. A random and severe electric shock that Holroyd suffers confirms that the day of judgment is near. Holroyd inadvertently worsens matters when he forbids Azuma-zi from going near the dynamo. The native construes this to be religious persecution and then imagines a new rhythm in the machine enunciating "four words in his native tongue" (80). The speaker, nevertheless, dismisses this as delusional. The incessant whirl and din of the dynamo shed, he ruminates, may have "churned up his little store of knowledge and big store of superstitious fancy, at last, into something akin to frenzy" (80).

An important turn in the psychic development of the believer comes when the machine "suggested to him" that he offer a blood-sacrifice to "the Dynamo Fetich," a delusion filling him with "a strange tumult of exultant emotion" (80). Blood sacrifice, Wells would write in 1921, is tied in with agriculture and is intended to propitiate the gods and to ensure an abundant harvest. In "Dynamos," on the other hand, the persecuted adherent solicits the deity for deliverance from a persecutor. Thus, the Lord of the Dynamo which Azumi-zi created is a vengeful, retributive, and redemptive deity—a defender of its nascent cult and of its solitary acolyte.

The electrocution of Holroyd, almost an anti-climactic event, confirms the dynamo's power and righteousness as it frees its votary from persecution. The workings of the religious intelligence, according to Wells's scheme, then become self-destructive. Azuma-zi's decision to murder Holroyd's replacement lacks ritualistic justification and is rationalized by the self-reflective question: "Was the Lord Dynamo still hungry?" (83). In the ensuing struggle with the new overseer, the Aborigine is electrocuted. The speaker concludes that the worship of the dynamo deity, though "the most short-lived of all religions," boasted of a martyrdom and a human sacrifice (84). This closing statement summarizes Wells's purpose: to demonstrate how primitive religion finds its genesis in awe, deprivation, and ignorance; how it can justify murder in the name of transcendent power; and how it can destroy its professor. Yet behind the satiric speaker who exposes and ridicules religion for being a delusive vice is the author who presents us with a fictional correlative to Edward Burnett Tylor's opinion on the religious impulse. Tylor wrote, in *Primitive Culture* (1871), that

> Few who will give their minds to master the general principles of savage religion will ever again think it ridiculous, or the knowledge of it superfluous to the rest of mankind. Far from its beliefs and practices being a rubbish-heap of miscellaneous folly, they are consistent and logical in so high a degree as to begin, as soon as even roughly classified, to display the principles of their formation and development; and these principles prove to be essentially rational, though working in a mental condition of intense and inveterate ignorance [II.16–17].

Thus, in "The Lord of the Dynamos," Wells depicts the consistency and internal logic of fetishistic religion, along with the rational principles and elements of its development. Azuma-zi's profound religious experience occurs, in Tyloresque terms, under duress and "intense and inveterate ignorance." The story traces the development of primitive religion from its psychological and behavioral inception, through a ritualistic stage, and finally to a stage culminating in homicide which was motivated by revenge, and by a desire for supernatural power and redemption.

"Jimmy Goggles the God" (late 1898) retraces the developmental stages of religion outlined in "The Lord of the Dynamos" but does not reach the sacrificial or retributive stage. The most intriguing aspect of

this story is that the sacrificial stage of the process has a historical referent in what could conceivably have been one of its sources: the murder
of Captain James Cook. I would like to explore this parallel.

The speaker, a salvage diver whose helmeted diving suit is affectionately dubbed "Jimmy Goggles," attempts to retrieve gold from the cap-
sized vessel *Ocean Pioneer*. Without warning, Papuans, a native black race
of New Guinea, attack the speaker's boat. The submerged diver survives
the attack, but his shipmates are brutally murdered. He emerges on the
beach, is confronted by the savages, and then inflates his suit defensively.
The speaker recounts how this inflation leaves the natives awe-struck:
some flee while others prostrate themselves (294). They begin a bowing
dance around the diver. The speaker recollects how "these poor, mis-
guided, ignorant creatures" conduct him to their place of worship where
their "joss" or idol is. There, they present him to the "old black stone,"
the focus of their monolithic religion. He uses this situation to his advantage. Understanding the depths of their "ignorance," he plays the part of
a god, howling "wow-wow" in baritone, swinging his arms around, while
ceremoniously turning their idol over and sitting on it (295). For the
diver, this is a desperate mime. But, for the believers, it signifies the dis-
placement of an inanimate fetish by an animate deity. So they worship
him.

Within the relative safety of the suit, the diver complains about the
heat, his fatigue, and the abominable practices of the natives as the frenetic worshipers burn offerings to their newly found god (295–96). The
lewd dance in his honor incenses him until, finally, he is left alone to
unscrew his window. Ironically, what the natives think is a deity is actually a famished survivor who cannot consume his own offerings (296). In
the morning, he resumes the role of "a god among the heathen," a role
temporarily preserving his life (297).

The Papuans consider these occurrences to have been the effects of
their worship—signs that the indwelling power of Jimmy Goggles is
pleased. As the tribal god of these "savages" for four months, the salvager
recollects a number of fortuitous events: how offerings coincided with the
winning of a battle, good fishing, an abundant crop, and even the capture of his own brig (297). For shelter, the diver tries to convince his worshipers to build him a "holy of holies," where he can safely disrobe. He
even resumes his salvage mission at sea, an activity convincing the natives
he is indeed a marine god (297).

When a missionary arrives to discover the diver and the revered diving suit, the speaker tricks him into bowing down under the pretense of
reading an inscription. To the natives who stand at a distance, this oth-

erwise meaningless gesture demonstrates Jimmy Goggles' primacy over Christianity because it appears as if the priest is bowing to the idol. After the diver manages to escape the Papuans, the natives are angry with the missionary who is blamed for having driven their god away (299).

Wells reveals throughout this story an informed understanding of how fetish religion develops and ingeniously demonstrates this through the salvager's experience. "Jimmy Goggles" is revered for having power over the elements: he can walk in and out of the sea (we willingly suspend our disbelief in this regard); for the native witnesses, the diving suit (like the dynamo for Azuma-zi) contains an indwelling power with authority over nature. Consequently, they hope to communicate with it through oblation and ritual. That Jimmy Goggles is thought to have been a marine god is significant since the natives depend upon the ocean. To worship such a deity, the natives think, will bring them into intimate contact with an intelligence in balance with, or in control of, oceanic elements and forces. The inclination to ceremonial worship, beginning with awe, turns quickly to systematic devotion as the tribe sequesters the deity in a sacred place and ensures its retention with sacrificial food. Since the worship of Jimmy Goggles provides the Papuans with a sense of control over refractory aspects of their environment, they believe that they can influence mundane events, such as wars and harvests, if they remain faithful devotees of the sea god. Yet the salvager (a pun on savior) is no anthropologist. He can only deride the cult. Thus, the Papuans are silly, ignorant, and stupid (297). The derision notwithstanding, "Jimmy Goggles" reflects Wells's astute understanding of how primitive religion originates and manifests itself.

Although "Jimmy Goggles" does not proceed to the sacrificial stage of primitive religion, Wells may have been thinking of James Cook's ill-fated voyage as a source for the story. It is difficult to say with any certainty that Wells was thinking of Cook's experiences in the South Pacific when writing "Jimmy Goggles." Nevertheless, one cannot ignore the parallel evidence.

Allan Villiers, upon whose biography of Cook I rely here, traces these extraordinary events. When Cook (1728–1779) arrived in Kealakekua Bay, Hawaii, on January 17, 1779, the Polynesians prostrated themselves before him, conducted ceremonies and processions, chanted and formally exchanged valuable gifts with the crew (258). Amidst this apparent adulation, Cook and his crew overheard what they thought to be the word "Orono" or "Rono" (259). Actually, the natives had been addressing Cook as "Lono," the Hawaiian god of agriculture who was honored by merry-making, idol worship, feasts, and sports (259). According to the myth,

Lono had inaugurated the festival by descending to earth on a rainbow in search of a wife (Carlyon 361). However, after his wife committed adultery, he beat her to death (361). Guilt and remorse over this act moved him to institute the festival in her honor. He is said to have departed Hawaii in a well-stocked canoe, promising that he would return there on a floating, forested island loaded with gifts (361). Lono, it appears, was a retributive, violent, yet magnanimous character.

In late 1778, islanders spread the word that great floating islands with masts like trees had indeed arrived (Villiers 259–61). On these floating islands were white men burdened with treasure, whom the natives described as having three-cornered heads (hats) and long hair; as breathing fire and smoke (pipes) (253); as taking objects out of their skin (jackets); as having horns (officers' felt hats); and as removing the tops of their own heads (wigs) (260). The islands, of course, were the H.M.S. *Discovery* and the H.M.S. *Resolution,* and the trees were their masts (261). They bore a considerable quantity of treasures for the Hawaiians, notably swine and dogs (both of which figured in the legend) (261).

Cook was hailed, therefore, as the exiled god Lono, the one who had prophesied his return to Mauai. Coincidentally, both Hawaiian tradition and contemporary politics made the return of Lono appear to be well timed: Kalaniopu, the king of Hawaii at that time, attributed Lono's arrival to a previous battle victory, and the god appropriately chose as his port of call, Honaunau, on Kealakekua Bay, the ancient city of refuge that the Hawaiians traditionally revered (Villiers 260).

Cook's history and Wells's fiction parallel each other closely at several points. The idea that the god's return will bring good fortune figures directly in "Jimmy Goggles." The diver recounts how his arrival coincided with the tribe's good fortune:

> I must confess that while I was god to these people they was extraordinary successful. I don't say there's anything in it, mind you. They won a battle with another tribe—I got a lot of offerings I didn't want through it—they had wonderful fishing, and their crop of pourra [edible root (Sherborne 527n.)] was exceptional fine. And they counted the capture of the brig among the benefits I brought 'em. I must say I don't think that was a poor record for a perfectly new hand. And, though perhaps you'd scarcely credit it, I was the tribal god of those beastly savages for pretty nearly four months [297].

In order to appease Lono-Cook and to maintain their spiritual authority and despotism, the chiefs and priests gave him conciliatory gifts (Villiers 260–1). The problem was that they had taken these goods from the poor who, bedazzled by the events at hand, at first readily complied. Ironically unaware of the real reason behind this adulation, Cook had no idea that these gifts consisted mainly of "priestly imposts taken from the people for the god Lono's happiness" (Villiers 260–1). So Cook found himself, inadvertently, as the focus of a political power struggle in Hawaiian society between the theocrats and the people. When the god of abundant harvests set sail, the local larders, gardens and pigsties had been seriously depleted, leaving the once-devout natives with a sense of betrayal and bitterness towards the god who was supposed to have delivered them from their deprivations (261).

When H.M.S. *Resolution* needed repairs, Cook had no choice but to re-anchor at Kealakekua (Villiers 262–6). But, upon returning, he found a disillusioned and hostile populous. They still believed him to be a god and his crew immortal, but that pretense would evaporate when members of Cook's crew died. The natives' bewilderment at this occurrence suggests a connection with *The Island of Doctor Moreau*, when Prendick struggles to explain away the deaths of Moreau, Montgomery, and M'Ling, and to preserve his authority (*M.Var.*67–9). For Cook, disaster loomed: a frenzied native crowd murdered him and his shore party, believing perhaps that they were assassinating a tyrannical deity (266-8). Whereas the salvage diver of "Jimmy Goggles," after witnessing the ferocity of the Papuans, maintained his ruse in order to survive, Cook died (some argue) without having realized that he had been taken for Lono. Cook's ill-fated return had been prompted by the pressing need to retrieve hull spikes that natives habitually stole (264).

Another circumstantial, although highly evocative, connection between Cook's last days and "Jimmy Goggles" involves the salvage diver's conflict with the missionary, who is about to reveal his presence to the Papuans. The diver, as we recall, tricked the missionary into a gesture of obeisance, which seemed to confirm the superiority of the oceanic mythology over Christianity. The departure (or escape) of the diver and the supposed bad fortune to follow are then blamed on the Christian missionary who remains behind. Perhaps this was Wells's way of vindicating Cook whose reputation had suffered posthumously at the hands of missionary writers. Some American missionaries, in particular, relying on Hawaiian oral tradition, had accused Cook of having played the role of Lono deliberately and for self-indulgent reasons (Hays xiii). This hypothesis contrasts ironically with the diver's motive: he played the god in order to survive. Either Cook lost his life because he was ignorant of the sociopolitical implications of the cult formed around him and was resented as an oppressor, or, as H. R. Hays suggests, because he exploited native myth and his place in it. There is some evidence that he had speculated on the meaning of taboo, so he had some knowledge of local beliefs; whether or not he respected them is a question that I cannot answer. In any event, the magnanimity of Lono-Cook faded before the hardship his adherents had caused in his name. The darker side of Lono, no doubt, gained prominence in the minds of the Hawaiians: here was a merciless husband, an insatiable tyrant, and a mortal being.

An interesting historical postscript is that the devout Hawaiians probably ate Captain Cook. After he was killed, his head and extremities were given to the chiefs while the remainder of his corpse was chopped up and distributed to the nobility who allegedly burned the parts (N. Davies 191). When the high priests insisted that ten pounds of Cook's flesh, along with some bones, ought to be handed over to the British, it was discovered that some of the tissue had been salted (N. Davies 191).

The genesis of primitive religion has a central role in *The Island of Doctor Moreau*, and this work further evidences the value of Wells's views on the subject. In a late 1894 revision of the text, as I pointed out in chapter 1, Moreau recounts to Prendick how he transformed an orangutan into his first "man" (*M.Var.*133). The creature, as Moreau's pupil, receives from his creator the basics in writing, reading, and math. Beginning with a clean mental sheet, it has no recollection of its simian past or of Moreau's physiological procedures. Because of its mild and abject demeanor, the Kanakas educate him, and he learns well (*M.Var.*133). With his ability to read, the orangutan acquires moral ideas.

Most importantly, one of Moreau's Kanaka crewman, "a bit of a missionary," teaches "the thing" to read, by implication, from the Bible (*M.Var.*133). In the main text, a humanized gorilla becomes the pupil of a Kanaka missionary. From him the gorilla-man also learns to read basically and absorbs moral ideas (*M.Var.*50). Once again, by implication, it is the Bible that is the reading text and the source of moral principles. This is an important point, for it identifies the source of the primitive religion on the island.

When Prendick witnesses a Beast-Folk ritual, he fails to recognize that their chants may be biblical in origin. I am referring particularly to the gorilla-man's references to "Allooloo & Klisling," which Prendick dismisses as gibberish. Robert M. Philmus successfully traces the Kiplingesque reference: "Allooloo," conjoined with the phonetic jumble of Kipling's name, derives from the anthropomorphic bear Baloo, who utters the mournful cry "Arulala! Wahooa" in *The Jungle Book* (*M.Var.*152–3n.). A secondary meaning also presents itself: "Allooloo" may be a corrupt form of "Alleleuia," the Vulgate transliteration of "Hallelujah," meaning "praise." "Alleleuia" is the form of doxology used in the fifth book of *Psalms*, as well as in *Chronicles*. The *Psalms* containing "Hallelujah" praise God for his power and wisdom in the creation of the world, and in the liberation of Israel from Egypt (*Psalms* 104, 105, 106, 131). Moreover, the *Hallelujah Psalms* (#146–150), as they are called, exalt God's blessings as being stronger and more efficacious than those that idols conferred (Hempel 115).

A tentative parallel materializes between the Israelites' relationship with God and that of the Beast-Folk with Moreau. Thus, along with the common recognition of omnipotence, comes the parallel that, as God delivered the Israelites from the bondage of theriomorphic religion in Egypt, Moreau delivers his creations from bestiality itself. A close reading of the text will support this comparison.

When the ape-man enjoins Prendick to say the "words," Wells is referring to the Ten Commandments, which literally means the "ten words." The Commandments of *Exodus*, Chapter 20, are God's vocal proclamation on Mount Sinai, written on two stones and given to Moses (*Exodus* 24:12, 31:18, 32:151; *Deuteronomy* 5:22, 9:10f.). The first five Commandments (*Exodus* 20:3–12) proscribe polytheism, idolatry, and the dishonoring of God's name; and they command the sabbath observance and the honoring of one's parents. Commandments six to ten (*Exodus* 20:13–17) sum up in negative terms the social and moral requirements of the Israelite community if it is to preserve holiness (Harrelson 569–71). Despite Prendick's deprecation of the Moreauvians' litany of the "words" as nothing more than an "idiotic formula" and "the insanest ceremony" (38), the litany actually demonstrates that the Beast-Folk have adopted a Judeo-Christian, juridical ethic.

Identifying transgressions against nature, society, and the godhead, the litany consists of two sophisticated formulae. Containing more than five prohibitions, the first formula is subdivided into three parts: an infinitive phrase identifies a transgression ("Not to go on all fours"); an independent clause asserts civic culpability ("*that* is the Law"); and an interrogative clause predicates one's humanity on adherence to the Law ("Are we not Men?"). The "words" that the Beast-Folk presumably derive from the orangutan's Bible study enunciate rightful behavior. Several proscribe predation, quadrupedalism, and (in paraphrase) promiscuity, whereas the injunctions (against going on all fours or sucking up drink) pertain to being herbivores. In effect, the Moreauvian ethic for moral behavior sets bipedal vegetarianism up as the ethical standard for island life.

The chant's secondary formula, containing seven indicative clauses, apotheosizes Doctor Moreau himself. He is believed to be omnipotent and to have dominion over the House of Pain where he re-combines natural forms and has the ability to create, to wound, and to heal; thus, his power transcends ordinary natural processes. In the second part of the formula, the litany ascribes the lightning, the sea, and the stars to his dominion. The anthropological significance of this experience, once again, escapes Prendick who derogates the ritualists as "grotesque caricatures of humanity" (39). He does not perceive that the islanders who assimilated the rudiments of Yahweh religion have fashioned a paternalistic and monotheistic cult, one that prefigures Wells's description, in 1920, of Neolithic religion. Truly a multi-specific society, Moreau's islanders share a common though flawed humanity. Despite their diverse and *sui generis* characters, they have combined to form a Neolithic culture with Moreau as a paternalistic demi-god, and with biblical texts as the source of their creed.

The anthropomorphic image is what they value, for each has been created in "god's" image. The fabric of this island's universe inheres in the being of Moreau, an incarnate god. Thus, when he is slain, the faithful are disoriented. The ape-man's crisis of faith is expressed interrogatively: "Is there a Law?"; and "Is it still to be this and that? Is he dead indeed?" (*M.Var.*68). At first, Montgomery and Prendick are hard-pressed to dissociate the creator from the Law, with which he was identified. The close association of Moreau with the Law is deeply ironic in that the former is not committed to it in any serious way. For Moreau, the Law is an efficient means of controlling the islanders. Of the cult and its beliefs, however, he knows little or nothing. He tells Prendick, for example, that the Beast-Folk live a mockery of rational life, and that "There's something they call the Law. Sing hymns about 'all thine'" (*M.Var.*51). Inasmuch as Moreau's interest in his creatures is purely physiological, he is insensitive to their cultural expressions. Unknown to him is the distinct possibility that the tutelage of the missionary Kanaka has had far-reaching effects, for the biblical laws of *Exodus* and of *Deuteronomy* have shaped the Beast-Folks' consciousness and religious culture.

Moreau underestimates the intelligence of his creations, and this factor erodes his authority. In the shaping of the Beast-Folks' consciousness, he implanted "Fixed ideas" in their minds (*M.Var.*52). In this way, they were hypnotized, having been told that certain things are impossible, and that certain things are strictly forbidden. However, if one considers the skeptical inquiry of the Satyr (an *ape*-goat [italics added]), one wonders if Moreau was absolutely successful in his mind-control efforts. In the primate mind especially, these safeguards cannot fully suppress rational thought. If Prendick is an incarnate deity (they ask), how can he weep and bleed? How can the Law persist if Moreau is mortal since he, in a pharaonic sense, enforces and embodies the code? And how can the whip-bearers succumb if they are demi-gods? Prendick's brilliant maneuver, probably the only available one in the light of these conundrums, is to disincarnate Moreau and turn him into a ubiquitous deity who "is not dead at all" (*M.Var*.68). He states that Moreau "has changed his body.... For a time you will not see him. He is—there [pointing upwards] ... where he can watch you. You cannot see him, but he can see you. Fear the Law" (*M.Var*.68). Prendick transmutes Moreau from incarnate demi-god into ubiquitous sky-god (could it be that Prendick recalls the formula in the ritual which speaks of Moreau's cosmic splendor and authority?). The ape-man, an austere adherent of the cult, accepts Prendick's theological pronouncement at face value, piously exclaiming that, "He is great, he is good"; and he then peers fearfully into the trees to where the spirit of Moreau has reputedly ascended (*M.Var*.68). To account for the deaths of Montgomery and of the Sayer of the Law, Prendick uses a similar tactic; but, in this instance, the Law itself, and not the person of Moreau, is ascribed the qualities of omniscience and of retributive power (*M.Var*.75).

The deifications of Moreau, Montgomery, M'Ling, and the Sayer of the Law show that Prendick, like the salvager, must improvise a myth in order to placate an otherwise bellicose native population.

The image of the Sphinx in *The Time Machine* has been interpreted in Sophoclean and Oedipal (Ketterer [340]; Scafella [255]), in socio-economic and historical (Stover 3), and in socio-biological terms (Prince 544-45). The image also has religious meaning but only if viewed in an Egyptian not in a Greek context. The connection of the Sphinx with a later passage on the Eloi's initial reaction to the Time Traveller suggests that Wells was also commenting on primitive religion and that, in addition to Sophocles, he had Egyptian civilization in mind.

General knowledge of Egyptian architecture helps us to understand the Wellsian Sphinx. Let us consider the Time Traveller's initial impression of the building:

> A colossal figure, carved apparently in some white stone, loomed.... It was very large.... It was of white marble, in shape something like a winged sphinx, but the wings, instead of being carried vertically at the sides, were spread so that it seemed to hover. The pedestal ... was of bronze ... the sightless eyes seemed to watch me; there was the faint shadow of a smile on the lips [*OTM* 21–2].

The Time Traveller's description, though impressionistic, highlights the most prominent features of the building: it is marble (as far as he could judge); it is sphinx-like, having a recumbent base, most likely in animal form; it has a weather-worn, human face; and it has horizontal rather than vertical wings (which suggests the Traveller was aware of traditional wing-motifs such as the vertical bird wings on the 16-foot Assyrian sphinxes guarding the Palace of Assurnasirpal II, in Nimroud Calah [884–859 B.C.]) (Myers 21, 30, 64, 139, 172, 186). The Traveller's observations, therefore, suggest some knowledge of the sphinx tradition, and especially of its mythic ramifications.

The Sphinx is foreboding, not because of its grotesque and heterogeneous features, but because it is emblematic, in the Traveller's view, of a rapacious civilization (*OTM* 22). Its pedestal, we recall, is made of bronze, a significant clue to the identity of its builders and to their cultural ethos. The Bronze Age, according to Wells, was the period when Neolithic religion and its horrible practices had reached their pinnacle. Could the civilization responsible for the Sphinx be in the midst of a Bronze Age comparable to that which began in the Middle East in 3500 B.C.? The Time Traveller, who is temporally disorientated, seems more inclined to accept the idea of the recurrence of an ancient technological civilization than of the idea that a future world is necessarily superior to a past one. All that he can be reasonably sure of is that the civilization responsible for the Sphinx is (or was) immensely powerful. From this perspective, he characterizes himself, diminutively, as "an old-world savage animal," an attitude suggesting that the Sphinx is an emblem of extant barbarism. Furthermore, he infers from the building that murder or even human sacrifice are practiced in this world. With respect to ancient Egypt, this intuition is not far afield. In *The Golden Bough*, Sir James G. Frazer writes that, at the grave of Osiris, the ancient Egyptians had burned red-haired men, and that their kings scattered the ashes with winnowing fans. The victims, Frazer conjectures, represented Osiris, the god of the corn harvest whose sacrifice and sowing would bring an abundant harvest (438–9). Osiris, as we recall, was one of the triumvirate of gods believed to be incarnate in the Pharaoh. According to Chapter LII of the *Book of the Dead*, men were indeed slain at the funerals of Osiris' followers (N. Davies 36).

If the Traveller is thinking of the Egypt (in the period from 2680 to 2565 B.C.), of the Sphinx, and of the Great Pyramid of Cheops at Gizeh, it is relatively easy to understand his reaction: the Egyptian Sphinx, which is a mythological construct, is sixty-six feet high, has the body of a lion, a human head, prognathous jaws, and savage eyes (Durant 139). We know that Wells appreciated Egyptian iconology, and especially the religious significance of architecture. In *The Outline of History*, he observes that the

Pharaoh was considered an incarnate god, specifically of a divine triad consisting of Osiris, of Hathor, and of Ammon Ra (or Re) (*OH*.I.227). Significantly, he makes this observation while discussing mortuary statues of the Pharaoh. In 1920, if not before, Wells rightly believed that Egyptian architecture had mythological significance. Sculptures and paintings, he explains, reinforced the idea that the Pharaohs were believed to be sons of the gods.

If the Sphinx of *The Time Machine* is observed from an Egyptian rather than Greek perspective, it suggests an Osiris-like myth for the 802nd millennium. Whereas in Greek mythology the Sphinx is a winged monster with the head and breasts of a woman and the body of a lion, the Egyptian Sphinx has a human male's head and a lion's body. And whereas the former is a destructive supernatural agent, the latter (at Gizeh) symbolizes the Pharaoh who is an incarnation of the solar god Ammon-Ra. Wells understood the hieratic character of Egyptian sculpture and art and that the identification of the king with these gods inextricably united solar and agricultural powers with the theocratic state (*OH*.I.221).

The Egyptian myth differs significantly from the story of Oedipus. In the Fifth Dynasty, the mythic relationship between the gods and humanity alternated between magnanimity and brutality (Carlyon 275). Ra created mankind, was incensed at human treachery, and then decreed that Hathor would exterminate his creatures (275). Having second thoughts, Ra restrained Hathor but with great difficulty; at this point, a redemptive phase began: Hathor, the destroyer of mankind, became wet nurse to the Pharaohs, and through this medium they imbibed divinity as a hereditary right (275). Henceforth, the Pharaohs claimed to be incarnations of their creator, Ra (275).

If we interpolate the Egyptian tradition into *The Time Machine*, the Sphinx will have more in common with the ideas of an incarnate solar deity and of a dynastic civilization proficient in the use of bronze and marble than with the demonic trickster of the Oedipal myth. Furthermore, if Wells's Sphinx is in the Egyptian rather than Greek mythological tradition, it is emblematic of overt power, both cosmic and mundane.

To which power or cultural heritage, either Eloi or Morlock, does the Sphinx belong? Because its visage, like that of its Egyptian counterparts some four millennia in our past, is weather-worn, and because the urban site where it rests is ruined, one suspects that it is no longer culturally extant. But it most certainly was of theocratic importance to the forebears of one of the two human species.

In view of the Sphinx's architectural and affective gravity, it is reasonable to infer that its builders and users are precursors of the Eloi rather

than of the Morlocks. Evidence supporting this premise exists in the second passage that I wish to elucidate. The Eloi's religious beliefs are conveyed to the Traveller who, like many of Wells's protagonists, fails to
appreciate their importance. One of the Eloi questions the Traveller about
his point of origin, that is, whether he descended "from the sun in a thun-
derstorm." He teases them, "point[ing] to the sun, and [giving] them ...
a vivid rendering of a thunderclap as startled them. They all withdrew a
pace or so and bowed" (24–5). Humored by the fact that these people
believe him to be an incarnate solar god, a veritable Pharaoh-Ra, the Time
Traveller stands before them, like Cook before the awe-struck Hawaiians. Exacerbating the Traveller's ignorance is his smug attitude: he dismisses the Eloi as retarded adults, insinuating that they will treat him like
a specimen, as a "plaything" (*OTM* 25) to be exhibited in the nearest
building. Perhaps he believes that the Eloi are the creators of the Sphinx,
understood in the Grecian sense of demonic trickster.

The effete Eloi contradict his preconceptions about intellectual history as a progressive development. What he has encountered is a primitive society, ostensibly of solar worshipers, who possess a messianic myth
(or the fragments thereof), comparable to the one surrounding the oceanic
god Lono. Their floral display and exuberance are genuine, for the Eloi
anticipated the advent of just such a solar entity who would arrive in a
storm. Failing to connect the Sphinx to the Eloi's behavior, the Traveller
does not consider that the solar religion resonating from the Sphinx is
extant in the mythology of the Eloi, whose religious sense far surpasses
that of five-year-old children. The tradition of solar worship links
pharaonic religion and the creators of the Sphinx, historically, to the Eloi
who retain vestiges of this once-sophisticated belief system.

The most interesting aspect of Wells's portrayal of primitive religion
in the imaginative literature is how effortlessly he interweaves anthropological theory into the fiction, even though the fiction antedates the fully
developed prose discourse of 1920. In "The Lord of the Dynamos" (September 1894), for example, we observe the gradual development of a fetish
cult originating in the mind of Azuma-zi, and its phases can be identified.
Thus, a vague sense of spiritual presence generates strong emotional
attachments, elicits intense reactions from the believer, and stimulates
him to undertake a number of complex activities, namely ritual devotion,
propitiation, and eventually the ritual sacrifice of a human being. Rather
than enumerate each phase in the genesis of Azuma-zi's religious thinking, Wells portrays its development subtly through the words of an omni-
scient, occasionally intrusive narrator. Mundane and trivial events, such
as Holroyd's misconceived comments, a gleam of light, and the tonal

modulations of the dynamo, contribute to the gestation of the religion in the mind of the oppressed believer.

In "Jimmy Goggles," a similar process unfolds. The fetishistic idolatry engendered in the Papuans moves from intense emotion (awe and fear) to ritual and sacrificial oblation. The difference between "Dynamos" and "Goggles" is largely perspectival. Whereas the reader scrutinizes Azuma-zi's religious development at one remove, in "Jimmy Goggles," this development is mediated by the salvage diver who, while inhabiting the fetish, assumes the role of the undifferentiated spiritual force and actually participates in the ceremonies to maintain his ruse. Ironically, in "Jimmy Goggles," the life of the "god" literally depends on the ignorance of the supplicants, whereas the supplicants believe that they depend upon the newly found god.

The historical parallel with the story of Captain Cook is revealing in this regard as well. One argument is that Cook (like the salvager) deliberately participated in the ruse of Lono-Cook for some vaguely self-aggrandizing reason. There is little dissent over the fact that the oppression of king and priest on that island contributed to the natives' hostility towards their redeemer, whose murder they may have thought a deicidal and even tyrannicidal act.

The theoretical rendition of primitive religion in *The Island of Doctor Moreau*, unlike that in "Jimmy Goggles the God," is entirely unmediated. The burden of interpretation, therefore, is on the reader with respect to the sociological history of the island, for neither Prendick nor Moreau seems to apprehend the extraordinary cultural significance of Beast-Folk ritual. Nor is Moreau able to recognize Bible study (through the Kanaka missionary) as the likely source of the Levitical code and of the patriarchal religion that they either dismiss or ridicule. And, finally, the reader must be a literary archaeologist in *The Time Machine*: terrestrial animism is a remnant of an antecedent form of pharaonic religion, complete with a monumental iconology.

10

Jean Auel's
The Clan of the Cave Bear:
"defining the point"

Jean Auel, unlike William Golding, rehabilitates the Neanderthal as a kind of human being whose dignity, for the better part of a century, had been degraded in scientific and creative writings alike. She represents the Neanderthal, not through heroic or pristine distortions, but by recreating the facts of this creature's life, according to the latest and most plausible scientific theories of her times. The virtue of Auel's work is its believability: paleoanthropological authenticity communicates the facts about these misunderstood early humans.

Since Auel achieves scientific fidelity in at least three salient areas— language, technology, and human evolutionary history—I would agree with Susan Isaacs who writes that the author skillfully weaves "her facts into the fabric of the book, providing texture as well as information" (14). Brian Stableford justifiably calls *Clan* an ingenious combination of "realism based in modern scientific understanding" and "robust literary romanticism" (895). I would like to survey those areas in the novel where her success is most evident.

Language

Recently, scholars investigating prehistoric language capacity have focused on the anatomy of the vocal tract, including the larynx ("voice box"), pharynx, tongue, and other structures (Leakey & Lewin [1992] 270; Laitman [1988] 539–40). This research relies on the fossil record and on comparative anatomy. The position of the larynx in the neck reveals how animals vocalize. For most mammals, the larynx is situated high in the neck, limiting the vocal capacity. But, in human beings, the larynx descended to a much lower position in the neck, enlarging the part of the voice box above the throat that is responsible for modifying sounds. A low larynx enables human beings to speak.

As far as fossil man is concerned, investigators of speech evolution have been unable to reconstruct the soft tissues of the larynx (the cartilage and membranes) that are not preserved in skeletal remains. So it has been difficult to visualize and to speculate on the prehistoric voice apparatus. But investigators have been able to extrapolate from the basicranium (the bottom of the skull and roof of the vocal tract) to get an idea of how these soft structures worked in relation to the throat and voice box. In 1971–72, Philip Lieberman determined that the voice box, connecting the mouth and nasal passages to the esophagus, is essential for producing the vowel sounds *a* ("ah"), *i* ("ee"), and *u* ("oo") (Campbell 286–8, 345–6), phonemes upon which modern language depends. In fact, these sounds, in combination with consonants, make language. According to Lieberman, early man (notably *erectus* and Neanderthal man) had limited speech capabilities. Lieberman and his collaborator, Edmund S. Crelin, based this conclusion on similarities between babies' skulls and those of both modern apes and prehistoric man (Leakey & Lewin [1992] 271). Using an endocast, Crelin reconstructed the vocal tract of the old man of La Chapelle-aux-Saints, hoping to approximate the position of the larynx. This clay model of the vocal apparatus, complete with soft tissues extrapolated from the basicranium, allowed Lieberman to determine its dimensions and compare these data to those of modern man. The researchers concluded that the Neanderthals not only spoke at a slower rate than modern humans but would have been unable to use in rapid combinations the vowel sounds *a, i,* and *u.*

These findings evidently are reflected in the speech patterns of Auel's Neanderthals. Her subtle observance of the Lieberman-Crelin hypothesis is an example of her general scientific fidelity. This hypothesis, along with its fictional correlative, proved to be neither absolute nor incontrovertible. In 1984, Jeffrey Laitman argued that the position of the larynx for some Neanderthals falls within modern range (20–7); the La Chapelle specimen, he concluded, is atypical (cited by Leakey & Lewin [1992] 270–71; Corballis 158–60). In 1983, Baruch Arensburg and Bernard Vandermeersch based their counter-theory on the discovery of a Neanderthal hyoid bone in a Kebara Cave (Mount Carmel, Israel) (Leakey & Lewin [1992] 272). The hyoid, a tiny U-shaped bone, connects muscles to the jaw, larynx, and tongue. Essential to human speech, it provides anatomists with an accurate description of the vocal tract. This anatomical landmark allowed scientists to determine that the Kebara hyoid was similar to that of modern man, undermining any theory on Neanderthal speech limitation founded on basicranial morphology. Richard Leakey and Roger Lewin, in 1992, offered a third alternative: changes in the upper respiratory tract of the Neanderthal (a cold-weather adaptation) and not vocal morphology reduced the Neanderthals' ability to produce a wide range of sounds (273). As we approach the fiction itself, we will find that Auel's research reflects the Lieberman-Crelin hypothesis; moreover, since she does not introduce material contradicting an evolutionary reason for Neanderthal speech limitation, we can say that her fiction also does not contradict the Leakey-Lewin hypothesis.

Auel treats two aspects of Neanderthal speech in her narrative: verbal deficiency (consonant with the Lieberman-Crelin hypothesis) and a putative sign-language system (based on primate research of the late 1960s and early 1970s). In the first place, Iza, the clan's medicine woman, can only use words selectively and emphatically, a condition alleged to have been typical of the classic Neanderthal who "could not articulate well enough for a complete verbal language" (*Clan* 21). In addition, the narrator observes that these primitive people had "undeveloped vocal organs" (28), along with phonemic disabilities consistent with the Lieberman-Crelin hypothesis. Ayla's name, pronounced "Eye-ya," for the Neanderthal shaman, Creb, becomes "Aay-rr," the vowel suffix being converted to a consonant because the "ya" sound cannot be articulated. Similarly, "Aay-lla," for Iza, can only be enunciated as "Eye-ghaa"; like Creb, she substitutes the phoneme "-ghaa" for the unpronounceable "-lla" (40). These instances of vowel elision are evidence of Auel's imaginative fidelity to the Lieberman-Crelin hypothesis.

The assumption that the Neanderthals developed sign language to compensate for putative vocal deficiencies has an indirect basis in the fossil record and in contemporary primate research. Auel's Neanderthals communicate more "with gestures and motions"—that is, with a fully-developed sign language, "rich with nuance" (*Clan* 21). Their "hand signals, gestures, [and] positions" reflect Neanderthal social life, along with their "intimate contact" and "established customs." And their "perceptive discernment of expressions and postures" is also quite sophisticated (38). Since textual evidence for sign language abounds (*Clan* 126, 358–9, 406–9, 412, 474–5), I will elucidate the scientific background upon which Auel evidently drew. In agreement with the established opinion, as of 1980, that the Neanderthals were fully sapient human beings, capable of hunting together, of creating technology, of participating in ritual, and of having a tradition and a social life, Auel introduces sign language as a logical probability. A human group performing complex activities such as cooperative hunting or ritual interment must have communicated by some other means if their speech was limited. Auel's attribution of sign language to her Neanderthals is, therefore, reasonable based on indirect interpretation of the fossil record.

An additional source of indirect evidence for Auel is primate research on sign language. In 1969, the experimental psychologists Robert and Beatrice Gardner taught sign languages such as Amelsan to chimpanzees. Washoe, Lucy, Lana and other chimpanzees developed working vocabularies of one to two hundred words and were able to distinguish grammatical patterns (Campbell 23; Leakey & Lewin [1992] 274). In light of this published data of 1969, the idea that Neanderthals communicated in elaborate, non-verbal ways is not farfetched in the least. Like the Neanderthals, chimpanzees lack the kind of pharynx that allows human beings to articulate vowels. As Bernard Campbell remarks, they communicate with visual rather than with auditory symbols (23).

Since Auel's portrayal of Neanderthal language capacity, in 1980, imaginatively coincides with the findings of Lieberman, of Crelin, and of the Gardners, she achieves a high degree of scientific fidelity. The 1983 Kebara hyoid and its implications, however, demonstrate that scientific inquiry, and the fiction emulating it, is subject to modification or to disuse. The anatomical similarity between the Kebara hyoid and that of modern humans suggests that the Neanderthals could speak as well as we do.

Technology

Another example of scientific fidelity involves Mousterian technology. Here, the scientific authority Auel is likely to have consulted is François Bordes (1919–1981), a French prehistorian who created a standard lithic typology comprising sixty-three tool types (Soffer-Bobyshev 97). Bordes' statistical interpretation of fossils, from two sites in Dordogne, France, identified distinct Neanderthal tool kits, such as the Denticulate Typical, the Mousterian of Acheulean Tradition, and the Charentian.

Auel's consistency in this area is exceptional. Her tool maker, Droog, whose profession is essential to the clan's survival as hunters, demonstrates his dexterity on an unshaped flint from which he rapidly makes pointed tools, scrapers, borers, and awls. The details of manufacture correspond to Mousterian tool industry. Using bone hammers and other specialized instruments, such as a "stone-shaper," he creates hand axes adapted for gripping, tapered knives (precisely serrated, notched, and pointed), and a small-toothed or "denticulated" saw, notched and angled to fit the hand. Other instruments include a convex, blunt-edge scraper (suited to woodwork and skinning), a spearhead, and an awl-borer. Droog's industry and Auel's scientific precision are apparent in this passage:

> With a small, slightly flattened round stone, Droog gently knicked off the sharp edge on one side of the first flake to define the point, but more importantly, to blunt the back so the hand-held knife could be used without cutting the user; retouching, not to sharpen the already thin sharp edge, but to dull the back for safe handling. He gave the knife a critical evaluation, removed a few more tiny chips, then, satisfied, he put it down and reached for the next flake. Going through the same process, he made a second knife [227].

Auel's details correspond to the contemporary fossil record and to its conventional interpretation. Early in the Würm glaciation, the chronological framework of the story, the Neanderthals developed the disk-core technique (Droog works on a "discoidal nucleus" [*Clan* 226]). The appearance of denticulated flakes is historically significant, having facilitated the transition from the hunting of small game to the organized capture of large animals such as the mammoth. It is no accident, then, that Droog is described as blunting the back of a "denticulated tool" (*Clan* 227). Auel shows that she is as much a student of Bordes as she is of Lieberman, of Crelin, and of the Gardners.

Hominid Evolution

A third extrapolative line assesses the genetic relation between the Neanderthals and early-modern humans. If we recall, Wells's view, distorted by the pseudo-science of the 1920s, was that the early-modern humans conducted genocide against the Neanderthals. Auel rejects this extirpation theory. She acknowledges the possibility that the Neanderthals may have drifted into extinction and that early-modern humans superseded them, but she also makes a case for their intermingling—and for the survival of the former in the gene pool. Her thinking reflects an ongoing debate. Christopher Stringer, an advocate of the "Out-of-Africa" or monogenesis theory, believes that the Neanderthals and early-modern humans were two distinct hominid lines that diverged from a common ancestor 200,000 years ago and that each was a separate species. Accord-

ing to Stringer, early-modern humans migrated from Africa into Europe
to replace archaic man (Stringer & McKie 54–64,117–19,142–48). An
alternative theory, called the multi-regional, holds that hominids originating in Africa gradually evolved into contemporary forms wherever they
lived throughout Europe. Although the Neanderthals became extinct,
they had continually interbred with early-modern humans (Wolpoff
62–108).

Auel's fictional interpretation corresponds to the multi-regional theory. Two interbred children are the products of rape: a Neanderthal,
Broud, rapes the early-modern human Ayla, who bears the male hybrid
Durc; and a raiding early-modern human rapes the Neanderthal Oda,
who bears the female hybrid Ura. Auel dramatizes the genetic compati-
bility of these populations in the fiction: they are conspecific. Her attention to anatomical detail is meticulous although her effort to blend ethnic
features is contrived. Born with a high forehead and round, modern skull,
Durc has a contemporary face (a small nose, a chin, small jaws, and a large
head not supported by heavy neck musculature [*Clan* 332]). Ayla eventually figures out that Durc combines Neanderthal and early-modern
human traits because Broud is the father (350–1). Ura resembles but is
not an exact replica of Durc: she is stockier (a Neanderthal feature) and
has the same forehead and nose as he, but she is chinless and prognathous
(Neanderthal features). Her neck, like Durc's, is longer than the neck of
the Neanderthal babies (386). Creb, the tribe's shaman, realizes that Durc
is a hybrid, and he understands that early-modern humans will supersede
his people: "The Clan is doomed, it will be no more, only her kind will
go on" (478). He reasons that there are most likely others like Durc and
Ura, "Children of mixed spirits, children that will go on, children that
will carry the Clan on" (478). It dawns on Creb that his kind will survive, not as a distinct population, but in the heritage of early-modern
humans. The extinction of the Neanderthals, according to Auel, is not
tantamount to their annihilation.

Auel's extinction scenario enriches her narrative with exciting credibility and a degree of prescience. In spring of 1999, the Portuguese archaeologist Dr. Joao Zilhao (and his team) discovered the remains of a
four-year-old child displaying the morphological characteristics of both
Neanderthals and early-modern humans. According to Erik Trinkhaus,
a paleoanthropologist, the specimen proves that the two hominid groups
regularly interbred over more than 20,000 years (Wilford [1999] 1). The
child's small teeth, sharply pointed chin, and red-ochre burial style are all
early-modern human characteristics. Moreover, a radio-carbon date of
24,500 years also points to early-modern humanity: these remains are

much younger than the last signs of the Neanderthal (Kunzig 74). But Trinkhaus also identifies their Neanderthal features: a chin that retreats behind the teeth and the limb proportions (shin-to-thigh-bone ratio), both of which suggest Neanderthal lineage.

Auel's adherence to legitimate scientific findings in language, in technology, and in human evolution endows her narrative with extraordinary realism. Beyond its imitative merits, *The Clan of the Cave Bear* contains a genuinely inventive element: the idea that the Neanderthals and early-modern man interbred with one another.

11

J.-H. Rosny-Aîné's
Quest for Fire:
The Archaic Twilight

To appreciate J.-H. Rosny-Aîné's achievement in the *Quest for Fire*, one must first determine the time frame of the narrative and then the identity of the human subspecies who are the protagonists of the story. The promethean aspect of *Quest for Fire* is explicit. Like Prometheus, the hominid Naoh will transform the lives of his people through the acquisition of fire. But, beyond that similarity, the parallel between the two figures does not bear up well. Raymond Dart named one of his fossil finds *Australopithecus prometheus* because he (erroneously) believed that this creature was the first user of fire. As it turned out, *Australopithecus prometheus* was neither thief, arsonist, nor revolutionary.

The fictive hominid Naoh (as the transposed letters suggest) may have more in common with Noah than with Prometheus. Like Noah, Naoh will receive a salvific gift, not from God in the form of an ark, but in the communication of fire technology which he receives from nearly extinct hominids called the Wahs. The gift of fire in the cold Paleolithic world, then, parallels the gift of the ark in the midst of the Deluge: Naoh's fire technology will save the genus *Homo*, just as Noah's ark ensured the survival of biblical mankind.

David Pilbeam's informative introduction to human evolution illuminates Rosny-Aîné's taxonomic and evolutionary ideas. Initially, one has to determine whether or not *erectus* (Dubois' missing link) co-existed with early-modern humanity. According to Pilbeam, in the second half of the Pleistocene Epoch, when early-modern man first appeared, only one species was present at any given time; hence, Dubois' *Pithecanthropus* was extinct before the advent of modern man. But he qualifies this statement, adding that the populations making up the prevailing species were never homogeneous, for they always demonstrated considerable regional variation (158). The idea of regional variation, then, could be used to explain the co-extension of dissimilar hominids in the story, all of whom are either variants of early-modern man or, by definition, intermediate links between *erectus* and *sapiens*. The fossil record, up to 1995 (despite its unevenness), suggests that *erectus* had been well established 1.6 million years ago but disappeared as a species by 200,000 years ago. In all likelihood, then, between 200,000 and 35,000 years ago, hybrid early humans with primitive and early-modern traits co-existed with one another. This is precisely the kind of world Rosny recreates.

According to reputable paleoanthropologists, two evolutionary paths for *erectus* were possible: either this hominid gradually became extinct and early-modern man supplanted him; or this form gradually evolved *into* early-modern man (Rightmire 265; italics added). In either case, the temporal corridor in which these beings lived, from 200,000 to 35,000 years before the present, becomes a fertile area of conjecture, for during this archaic twilight, intermediate forms or missing links were likely to have shared the savanna with their genetic relatives, the African brethren of the Cro-Magnons. Rosny-Aîné, in 1911, anticipates the hypothesis (incrementally substantiated from the 1920s to the present) that certain *erectus* populations evolved into *Homo sapiens sapiens* during a 160,000 year period in the late Paleolithic Epoch. This is why the possession of fire is so salient to the story: through the technology of fire, the Oulhamrs will avoid extinction and eventually evolve into early-modern humans.

Rosny's description of the Oulhamrs, although impressionistic and incomplete, supports my contention that they are intermediate forms between *erectus* and archaic moderns. They are described as having "fine stature," suggesting upright posture and bipedalism, a trait common to both *erectus* and to *sapiens* (14). Rosny's hominids have "heavy faces" or prominent maxillofacial bones and musculature; their "low crania" mean that their foreheads are recessive (a primitive element), while their jaws are "fierce," evoking robustness (a herbivorous but also primitive feature). Their overly developed olfactory sense, which is incongruous with stereoscopic vision, is considered a primitive trait.

The only anatomical referent at Rosny's disposal, and one that he probably had in mind, was the rather subjective sculpture of Dubois' hominid on display at the Paris Exhibit in 1901. The more abundant and diversified specimens from Southeast Asia and China were to be discovered in the 1920s. If we compare the later information with Rosny's imagery, it becomes evident that the fictive hominid anticipates the anatomy of *erectus*: the later crania would present with a low profile, a flattened forehead, and a heavy face; the neck musculature and the cranial bones (a bulge at the mastoid angle and strongly developed crests) were therefore primitive features consistent with Rosny's portrait; and the "fierce" jaw of *erectus* was as robust as that of Rosny's creature and lacked any noticeable chin eminence (Rightmire 263). Furthermore, the Oulhamrs ("Old Hammerers" or ancient tool manufacturers, as the name suggests) have sapient attributes. They have the intellectual capacity to adapt to their environment and to learn from more advanced people. Their capacity for language, for tool technology, and for the opportunistic use of fire identify them with the lineage of modern man on the later Paleolithic continuum.

Intellectually (not physically) superior to the Oulhamrs, the Wahs are archaic sapiens. The former have a sophisticated tool technology similar to that of later Paleolithic cultures, characterized by blade industries, end-scrapers, burins, awls, spears and other projectile points, and perhaps even by the use of bows and arrows. Adept at hunting, at fishing, and at direction finding, the Wahs do indeed manufacture projectile weapons and have the controlled use of fire (113). It is the fire capability, beyond any other impetus, that galvanizes them culturally. With the hearth as the focal point of their gatherings, they socialize, chant, and tell stories, as did early-modern man of the later Paleolithic Epoch (113). Social interaction around the fire, it is important to observe, is a behavior distinguishing the Wahs from the Oulhamrs who tend to be solitary foragers, not communal hunters. The Wahs benefit from fire in many ways: it provides warmth and light; it tenderizes and detoxifies food; it drives away predators and pests; and it improves wood-working capabilities (Toth & Schick 208). The Oulhamrs master the techniques of fire making which the Wahs voluntarily hand on to them, and this technological transfer will direct the evolutionary impulse of Naoh's clan away from extinction and towards the sapient lineage.

Rosny realized that the evolution of the missing link from the *erectus* to the human lineage, along with being a genetic, morphological, and cultural progress, was also a mental development, reflected in the Oulhamrs' conceptualization of fire. Before they acquire control over fire, they depend upon its chance, environmental manifestations. Since they are opportunists in this regard, they are powerless; and powerlessness, in turn, makes them fearful. Rosny's use of figurative language conveys the cultural ethos of the Oulhamrs and their natural vulnerability. For them, the origin and composition of fire is mysterious, and they perceive it to be an organic entity with paradoxical properties. But, when they have fire control, the mystery will be dispelled, and they will no longer feel subservient to unseen, elemental powers. Ironically, metaphor, personification, and symbol are emblematic in the story of a primitive, pre-technological mentality.

Rosny's use of figurative language is especially revealing. The narrator recounts how, to the Oulhamrs, fire is a living thing, a kind of guardian that shelters, feeds, and guides them in their migrations across rivers and swamps. Fire protects them, driving off predators such as the bear, tiger, and leopard; and, though disincarnate, it is itself a mighty predator, for its flames are "red fangs" (11). The "source of all delights," fire makes meat more appetizing (and more nutritious) and also hardens tools and spearheads. Not only does it provide warmth and security, but it also reassures the band through its travels over savanna, cave, and forest. More than a utilitarian commodity, it is a procreative and redemptive entity: "father, guardian, and saviour" (11). Yet, despite these exalted attributes, it remains a protean phenomenon. Though a guardian, it can be ferocious, insatiable, and terrifying, especially when it escapes from its "cage" and consumes the trees (11).

Fire is also a voracious and indiscriminate beast, capable of destroying its tenders (11). Before the embers in the third cage go out, the dying flame is described as "an animal that is sick" (12). On other occasions, it is a beast of prey, feeding on branches, dry grass, and grease. As it feeds, it grows just like an animal would. Fire even has a life cycle: like living things, it replicates itself or increases in volume before dying (40). Yet fire does not behave according to the laws of organic growth: its stature is virtually unlimited; and, while it can be cut in two endlessly, "each piece will live." It also has the fantastic ability to contract and expand. When unfed, it will become an ember. When fed, it can become "as vast as a swamp" (40). It remains protean: "an animal" yet "not an animal." It has the capacity of swift locomotion, like an antelope, even though it has neither paws nor a crawling body. It has no wings, but it can fly; no mouth, but it can growl and roar. Nor does the lack of hands prevent it from taking possession of "wide expanses." These contradictory traits understandably perplex Naoh, who loves, hates, and reveres fire. The hatred stems from having been burned and from fire's unpredictability: it readily devours those who sustain it, and it is more cunning and ferocious than the fiercest predator. Yet its presence is nonetheless a "delight." A naturally occurring enigma, the devourer, as it is called, also brings comfort on cold nights and repose to the exhausted (40).

When their remaining fire is extinguished, the Oulhamrs find themselves dispossessed and disorientated. The dark and unfamiliar landscape
oppresses them. Early on in their odyssey, Naoh, Nam, and Gaw feel its
absence acutely: "accustomed to bonfires at night which were like barriers of light set against the sea of shadows," they became aware of their
"puniness." Without fire, they are defenseless against large predators, such
as the gray bear, the tiger, the leopard, or the lion, and stampeding herbivores can easily trample them. Moreover, they must eat raw meat, which
is a "gloomy meal," for "they loved the smell of roast meat" (21). The lack
of fire creates acute suffering, especially on dark moonless nights since they
are naturally diurnal creatures. Once again, the darkness "weighed them
down and engulfed them" (34). The hope for spontaneous combustion is
unfulfilled. Their weakness and the immensity of the unilluminated environment "crushed their spirits" (34).

Along with the figurative and mythic aspects of their fire culture, the
Oulhamrs and related groups have developed a technique for fire tending. When Naoh acquires a fire cage from the Kzams, he finds that they
sustain it in a nest of bark, "reinforced with flat stones." The skillfully
manufactured cage is composed of "a triple layer of schist held together
on the outside by oak bark"; because it is tied together with flexible
branches, it can be carried (75). Constantly vigilant, the Kzams protect
the flame against rain and wind and make sure that it neither smolders
nor flares (75). To maintain the proper height and intensity of the flame,
the specifications of which "millennial experience" has fixed, they know
precisely how much bark is needed (75). Furthermore, fire tending has
its own protocol, and skilled craftsmen are entrusted with this sacred duty.
Naoh, like the Kzams, is familiar "with all the rites transmitted by his
ancestors" (75). These rites taught him how to revive and sustain the fire.

The incendiary cultures of the Oulhamrs and of the Wahs intersect
at this point in the narrative. Naoh boasts to the Wahs of his ability as a
fire tender, but they are unimpressed (110). Concluding incorrectly that
the Wahs are an ignorant breed, he proudly offers to demonstrate how to
rekindle a dying flame. At this critical point in the narrative, he happens
to notice a woman igniting a fire with two stones (110). A commonplace
to the Wahs, this simple activity astonishes Naoh, for he believes that
combustion is somehow inherent in the stone. Fearful and slow to understand the process, Naoh eventually grasps that friction creates the sparks
responsible for the fire. The Wahs teach him to use the stones, and, when
he succeeds, he realizes that "he had just won something more potent than
any of his ancestors had possessed and that now the fire would be forever
his" (114).

That the phenomenon of fire occurs naturally and does not need to be retrieved, stolen, or cultivated, eludes Naoh for the moment. But the possession of the striking stones, in the context of Oulhamr history, proves to be a watershed event, nonetheless. On the eve of his return to the tribe, however, Naoh is not thinking about the future. His more mundane and self-serving thoughts have to do with his new status in the tribe, and with his capacity to instill fear in challengers. Above all else, he has his social status to consider: he will receive a wife, as was promised for succeeding in the quest, and he will become ruler after Faouhm. Even though his thoughts are shallow (127), from an evolutionary standpoint, his efforts to consolidate his authority will set a precedent for tribal solidarity and facilitate the transition from the hunter-gatherer way of life to that of the settled community. The controlled use of fire will bring this process to fruition in the long run.

Naoh has delivered his languishing kinsmen from darkness and fear (138). Since their loss of fire, the Oulhamrs lived in a state of perpetual anxiety, never ceasing to hold their weapons at the ready; thus, "fear and strained attention harassed their brains and bodies" (138). The sight of the ignited brand evokes gestures of humility and of acclamation from them (141). Naoh allows his kinsmen to resume the opportunistic lifestyle of the hunter-gatherer, but, out of "distrust and guile," he temporarily keeps the secret of the fire stones to himself (142). This, however, is a risky decision, the fullest implications of which he may not have realized. His coveting of this technology places the Oulhamrs in evolutionary jeopardy, inasmuch as the controlled use of fire is the key to their naturally selective advantage. If he were to die, his secret would die with him; consequently, the tribe and the entire subspecies could remain as unproductive hunter-gatherers.

But why does Naoh hesitate in communicating this discovery? He certainly intuits the importance of fire to Oulhamr longevity: "time without end" expands before him and Gammla, his spouse. Rosny's point here, which is beyond the heroic Oulhamr's ken, is that the secret of the iron pyrites, when handed down to posterity, will ensure the evolution of *erectus* into *sapiens* (143). Naoh does realize that, in the tribe's present state, they must be satisfactorily enlightened before they can accept this technological endowment, for the knowledge of combustion can easily be lost in the midst of tribal feuding. The Oulhamrs must emulate the archaic Wahs, for whom artificial ignition is a utilitarian activity. Significantly, Naoh intuits that striking up a fire will promote cultural life. The fire is conducive to socialization and to communication which, in turn, will transmit tribal characteristics from one generation to another through oral tradition, art and sculpture, and craftsmanship.

We are left with the question: is *Quest for Fire* an adumbrative and inventive text? Scientists in Rosny's day suspected that early-modern humanity (the Wahs) had the controlled use of fire. Given that suspicion, then Rosny's innovation is twofold. First, he postulates correctly that intermediate forms of hominids were co-extensive with early-modern man and that these creatures, though hybrids, were closer to modern man than to the extinct *erecti* that lived about 1,600,000 years before the present. Second, he infers correctly that the opportunistic use of fire preceded its controlled use and, therefore, that the more primitive beings—the links between *erectus* and *sapiens*—had gradually acquired the intellectual ability to apprehend pyrite technology. The Oulhamrs who occupy the archaic twilight between *erectus* and *sapiens* are entirely plausible creations. The most inventive aspects of *Quest for Fire* are the ideas that *erectus* evolved into *sapiens*, and that fire was the catalyst of this profound, prehistoric event.

12

H.G. Wells's
The Time Machine:
The Days of Triumph

In *The Time Machine*, H. G. Wells explores theoretical territory outlined in the early scientific discourse and, as David C. Smith writes, puts "evolutionary theory into fictional practice" (48). A central theme of the novel is human evolution. Perceiving this, John Huntington likens the Time Traveller and the reader to "evolutionary biologists," who want to distinguish one species from the other, and "to reconstruct the evolutionary sequence that links them" (42). In the construction of this sequence and of its aftermath, Wells surveys the descent of man over 30,000 millennia. His periodical scheme for geological time is tripartite: in the first phase (at some point before A.D. 802,701), *Homo sapiens sapiens* becomes extinct; in the second, two sub-species of his descendants subsist symbiotically; and, in the third (30 million years into the future), the human lineage has no heirs. Witnessing the bifurcation of the human species in the second phase, the Traveller participates directly in the interaction between the Morlocks and the Eloi. Although the ironic implications of his experience perplex him, he nonetheless manages to recount the events surrounding the descent and ultimate extinction of man.

The Time Machine accurately imitates established biological principles and phenomena, namely speciation, mutation, natural selection, symbiosis, and extinction, and is quintessentially inventive in its application of these scientific principles, mechanisms, and processes to man himself. The extrapolation of the natural history of man along a plausible evolutionary path, then, is the source of the novel's inventiveness.

In part one of this chapter, I trace Wells's thinking on the capacity of geographical isolation, of mutation, and of natural selection, to engender new species; in part two, I discuss his portrayal of the symbiotic interval of the 800th millennia, as well as the Traveller's ambivalence with respect to the ironic features of this condition; and, in part three, I consider Wells's vision of human extinction 30 million years into the future.

Isolation and Speciation

Wells was familiar with the writings of contemporary biologists who debated how isolation affects the evolution of animals and plants. In the *National Observer Time Machine*, he expresses his interest in the relationship between the geographical segregation of population and the development of distinct species. With respect to the Morlocks and the Eloi, the Time Traveller states that "a species may split up into two without any separation into different districts" (*DTM*.171); this theory is a central motif of *The Time Machine* as the Morlocks and the Eloi occupy disparate niches within a common district.

Further on, he credits John Thomas Gulick (1832–1923), a biologist, for having "worked out" the idea that an isolated district can promote the multiplication of species (*DTM*.171). In two influential papers, "On diversity of evolution under one set of external conditions" (1873) and "Divergent evolution through cumulative segregation" (1891), Gulick identifies the distinctive characteristics of *Achatinella* snails in different valleys on the island of Oahu, Hawaii, as evidence of micro-geographical variation (Mayr [1965]:204, 301, 310). He conjectures that, if human populations are separated from one another along linguistic, national, social, or educational lines, the evolutionary fission of the human race is a distinct possibility (Philmus *EW*.85–6n). The emerging species, because of its segregation from the original group, would have undergone genetic changes extensive enough to prevent its members from inter-breeding with its progenitors.

Gulick and others amended Darwin's idea that natural selection is the primary force behind speciation. In 1844, Darwin did not discount the effect of isolation on natural selection: "In a country ... undergoing changes, and cut off from the free immigration of species better adapted to the new stations and conditions, it cannot be doubted that there is a most powerful means of selection, *tending* to preserve even the slightest variation" that contributes to the survival of "organic beings" ("Essay of 1844" 241; italics in the original).

Other scientists who agreed with Gulick were emphatic about the role of isolation in the evolution of species. Moritz Wagner, in *Migrationsgesetz den Organismen* (1889), contended that geographic isolation and speciation were causally related, an opinion he based on the observation that the closest relatives of a species were usually found in adjacent areas and that geographical barriers separated them from other species (Mayr [1965]:480). Darwin, in 1859, revised his opinion on isolation but, once again, remained vague about its actual effects: it is an "important element in the modification of species through natural selection"; but, citing Wagner, he explicitly denies that it is "necessary" to the formation of new species ([1872] 79). The entomologist Karl Jordan (1861–1957) eventually corroborated Gulick's findings in the paper "On mechanical selection and other problems" (1896). While Darwin obtusely acknowledged that isolation is conducive to speciation, Jordan was more convinced of the causative relation between them; the latter arises, Jordan felt, if isolating factors provide a matrix for genetic changes (Mayr [1965] 480). Others dispel any doubt about causation in this regard and corroborate the work of Gulick, of Wagner, and of Jordan. For Theodosius Dobzhansky (1940–75) et al., geographic isolation is essential to the development of genetically distinct organisms, that is, of Mendelian populations "between which the gene exchange is limited or prevented by reproductive isolating mechanisms ... [or by] any genetically conditioned impediment to gene exchange between populations" (79). And Ernst Mayr maintains that reproductive isolation regularly occurs in segregated niches (*biotopes*) within a common territory or region, such as an island or a mountain ([1965] 556; [1982] 412–13, 562–65).

Wells explores the geographic-isolation theory in *The Time Machine*. Reading *The National Observer* variant in terms of this theory suggests that, at some time within a span of 10,000 years (A.D. 12,203), the Morlocks and the Eloi issued from a common ancestry (*DTM*.160). Here, the Time Traveller hypothesizes that the condition of geographic isolation may have had a socio-economic origin: the laborer and the indolent rich were separated from one another completely, thus inhibiting inter-marriage and gene exchange (*DTM*.167–8). The biological ramifications of this phenomenon are outlined, to a greater extent, in the "Atlantic" edition of *The Time Machine*. According to the Traveller, the two species, divaricating from the twentieth-century type, can be traced back 800 millennia to the separation of capitalist and laborer in nineteenth-century Britain. Industry and labor, he conjectures, had likely gone into subterranean factories, while the richer population sequestered itself on the surface (*OTM*.49). Socio-economic barriers led to reproductive isolation and eventually to the independent evolution of each group. The separation between classes, as the "key to the whole position" (*OTM*.49), precluded inter-marriage, and each population evolved along its own trajectory: "above ground you must have had the Haves, pursuing pleasure and comfort, and beauty, and below ground the Have-nots, the Workers getting continually adapted to the conditions of their labour" (*OTM*.50).

In his early writings, Wells considers factors stimulating the emergence of new species. "The Influence of Islands on Variation" (17 August 1895) exhibits Gulick's influence explicitly: "Isolation on islands," writes Wells, "has played a larger part in the evolution of the animals and plants than is usually attributed to it"—an opinion he bases on the observation that "an immense number of new species" periodically occur in such an environment (*A.40;EW*.235). As far as mankind is concerned, however, speciation is unlikely in view of human evolutionary history over the last twenty-five thousand years. He applies this idea to mankind in "The Rate of Change in Species" (December 15 1894): man is a slowly breeding creature, in whom "the evolutionary process must be almost stagnant, so far as the natural selection of non-acquired variations goes" (*EW*.129). Consequently, over thousands of years, humankind has not changed anatomically. In the essay "Human Evolution as an Artificial Process" (October 1896), Wells recapitulates the idea that the human species has remained physically unchanged since the age of "unpolished stone" (more precisely, since the later Paleolithic period, 10,000 to 60,000 years ago) (*M.Var*.191). In the *National Observer* variant, the Traveller poses this question: "Were you to strip the man of to-day of all the machinery and appliances of his civilisation, were you to sponge from his memory all the facts which he knows simply as facts, and leave him just his coddled physique, imperfect powers of observation and ill-trained reasoning power, would he be the equal in wit or strength of the paleolithic savage?" (*DTM*.166). Wells answers this question in "Human Evolution": transport the child of civilized, modern parents to a Paleolithic mother, and the child would grow up a savage. For the evolutionary distinction between the later Paleolithic and the Holocene or Recent Epoch is measured in intellectual not anatomical terms (*M.Var*.192). Together, early-modern and modern man have for millennia remained "a type of animal more obstinately unchangeable than any other living creature" (*M.Var*.193). Surveying this subject in the 1897 essay "The Acquired Factor" (9 January 1897), he suggests that, both anatomically and instinctively, the human race is no longer evolving although man's "mental environment" continues to do so. *Homo sapiens sapiens* can overcome his brutish ancestry through science, education, and art (*A.2;EW*.230): the "civilizing process" transforms the "natural man" into a creature "of tradition, suggestion & reasoned thought" (*M.Var*.193).

Although man has been "obstinately unchangeable" over thirty thousand years, Wells considers how isolation may initiate the multiplication of the human species. This condition certainly has brought about variation within the human community. In *The Outline of History* (1920), he remarks that, "whenever a body of men has been cut off, in islands or oceans, by deserts or mountains … it must have begun very soon to develop characteristics, specially adapted to the local conditions" (*OH.I.*131). But human isolation has itself been a rare event: a "wandering and enterprising animal," man has encountered "few insurmountable barriers." Ironically, human socialization and conflict have actually inhibited the multiplication of the human species: "Men imitate men, fight and conquer them, interbreed, one people with another." Whereas one impulse separates men into a "multitude of local varieties," another blends these varieties "together before a separate species has been established" (*OH.I.*131). The process through which speciation occurs, however, requires far more than a mere 25,000–year period (from the appearance of Neolithic man to the twentieth century). At present, the prospect of genetic differentiation is unlikely (*OH.I.*136). Rather, advanced civilization and culture are what truly define modernity. If progress is involved in the transition from one epoch to a succeeding one, it works only on the "social body," and it constitutes an "evolution of suggestions and ideas" (*OH.I.*189).

Wells and his co-authors, in *The Science of Life* (1929), acknowledge how important geographic isolation is to speciation and assert that this is "one of the everyday facts of systematic biology" (*SL.*618). Although natural selection "gives a satisfactory explanation of all evolution that is advantageous," it does not explain why some differences between "closely related creatures do not appear to confer any biological advantage at all" (*SL.*617). And although variations such as these can be neutral, having no clearly adaptive value, it is true that "mere geographic separation certainly helps in the development of difference" (*SL.*617). One reason for the proliferation of varieties in an isolated species is that it does not "intercross" with others of its kind on distant islands; consequently, each stock remains "free to develop along its own line."

Symbiosis

In *The Time Machine*, Wells establishes three pre-conditions for the emergence of new human species: (1) a lengthy time span (800 millennia); (2) the segregation of two branches of the human community within a common district but in self-contained niches (thus precluding gene exchange between the terrestrial and subterranean populations); and (3) the consequent evolution of each group along its own trajectory, demonstrating the effect of natural selection in the adaptation of each population to its unique circumstances. Wells introduces a fourth aspect of man's descent, one that is also an effect of natural selection. Even though the two populations have evolved into discrete, genetically incompatible human species, that does not preclude their symbiotic interaction—that is, "the mutually beneficial" interdependence "of different species" ("Symbiosis" 1158).

By A.D. 802,701, human evolutionary history has reached a point of equilibrium, at which the segregated human populations have come to depend upon each other symbiotically. This interdependence, however, should not be mistaken for a deliberate accord; rather, as the product of unconscious processes, it is amoral and ephemeral. The influence of Huxley, in this regard, is unmistakable. Wells elucidates two laws of evolution in his *Textbook of Zoology* (1898) (a later version of the 1892 *Textbook of Biology*): the law of inheritance and that of variation (Smith 19). The latter demonstrates that "the world is not made dead like a cardboard model or a child's toy, but a living equilibrium; and every day and every hour, every living thing is being weighed in the balance and found sufficient or wanting" (cited by Smith 20).

Wells, in the 1890s, was certainly aware of the phenomenon of symbiosis. As early as October 1892, in "Ancient Experiments in Co-operation," he observes that for nearly a decade scientists had been gathering evidence of "two *dissimilar* organisms [merging] together for their mutual benefit." This eventuality is unlike the idea of "destructive competition between individuals" (*EW*.190), thought to have been the principal evolutionary drive. The chief formulators of the idea of "destructive competition," of course, were Charles Darwin and Alfred Russel Wallace. Darwin, in 1844, wrote that "there is a recurrent struggle for life in every organism, and that in every country a destroying agency is always counteracting the geometrical tendency to increase in every species" ("Essay of 1844" 138). Wallace re-states this principle in "On the Tendency of Varieties to Depart Indefinitely from the Original Type" (1858): "The life of wild animals is a struggle for existence. The full exertion of all their faculties and all their energies is required to preserve their own existence and provide for that of their infant offspring. The possibility of procuring food during the least favourable seasons, and of escaping the attacks of their most dangerous enemies, are the primary conditions which determine the existence both of individuals and of entire species" (338).

Wells, it seems, did not repudiate the thesis of Darwin and Wallace;

instead, to articulate a fuller explanation of speciation dynamics, one that could be applied to the idea of human evolution, he accommodated Gulick's isolation theory to theirs. This synthetic maneuver envisages closed environments or *biotopes* (within a common district) in which mutations, both neutral and positive, can become more readily established in the gene pool of a species.

In the 29 August 1895 essay "Bio-Optimism," Wells suggests that the survival instinct reveals itself in a multiplicity of ways, some of which can be unexpected and subtle. For example, one fungus can struggle against another by arming itself with "an auxiliary alga" while man himself can refrain from killing cattle on sight to preserve them for his own convenience (*EW*.208). In this early context, Wells also refers to "Symbiosis" as simply another means of survival, one as valid as the struggle for existence (*EW*.208). The symbiotic phenomenon receives further attention in a later text. Using the lichen and other organisms as illustrations, Wells and his co-authors, Sir Julian S. Huxley and G. P. Wells, in *The Science of Life* (1929), begin by succinctly defining symbiosis: "This term (which is Greek for 'living together') is applied to cases in which two organisms of different kinds live in intimate union, and to the benefit of both" (*SL*.294). This intimate co-operation is, foremost, a matter of survival: "the struggle for existence forces them into … mutually helpful partnership[s]" (*SL*.922). It is also the result of natural selection: "Mutual partnerships are adaptations as blindly entered into and as unconsciously brought about as any others" (*SL*.932). A precarious equilibrium, symbiosis can be maintained "only by proper regulation and often elaborate adjustment" (*SL*.932). It may readily "over-balance and change into something different and even opposite" (*SL*.936), perhaps into mutual antagonism leading to the extinction of one or both of the symbionts. Thus, the "joint life" (*SL*.923) that symbiosis affords to two or more different species, as a coercive, unstable, and highly mutable arrangement, may degenerate into parasitism or predation.

Wells et al. point out that, although symbiosis is ephemeral and inherently unstable, it is not a "haphazard" occurrence (*SL*.928). On the contrary, as the product of natural selection, it benefits each principal, enhancing survival and increasing the likelihood of procreation; in this way, each species benefits but always in a fragile balance (*SL*.932). An undercurrent of "hostility" is ever-present, for an environmental or biochemical change in an organism or in its environment could upset the mutually beneficial balance.

Using the example of the interaction between a flatworm, *Convoluta roscoffensis*, and a single-celled green alga, Wells et al. demonstrate how "hostile symbiosis" operates. The relationship between these organisms is definitively symbiotic: the larval worm, having swallowed some of the algae, feeds normally on external nourishment until it reaches full growth, at which point it digests the algal colony in its gut. Up to that point, the algae simultaneously benefit from their existence inside the worm since they feed off of the animal's nitrogenous waste, and since they were exposed to ultraviolet light (necessary to their carbon dioxide metabolism) when the flatworms migrate periodically to the surface of the water (*SL*.933). Paradoxically, this symbiosis has heteronymous, parasitic, and predatory features. First of all, to set the process into motion, the larvae lure the algae to them using nitrogen as bait. The algae, though they benefit from life in the worm's gut, behave parasitically inasmuch as they flourish within, and at the expense of, the host. Conversely, in devouring its partner, the mature host is predacious. Wells's point is that biological reciprocity need not be absolutely equitable or homogeneous. The symbiotic cycle of the flatworm and algae is a well-chosen example: it depends upon an initial, predatory phase (on the part of the larvae); it exhibits parasitic features (on the part of the intestinal algae); and it eventually degrades into predatory activity (as the adult worm digests the internal symbiont).

The authors then apply this natural phenomenon, analogically, to the practice of animal husbandry: "The relation [of flatworm and algae] is like that between man and some animal which he would take into captivity only to fatten and kill, leaving the supply to be renewed by natural reproduction" (*SL*.933). According to this analogy, man is as parasitic in the drinking of cow's milk as a vampire bat or a mosquito is in sucking the blood of the very same cow; similarly, the slaughter of livestock for food suggests that man is a systematic predator. But the domestication of cattle for milk (e.g., Holstein-Friesian, Jersey, Guernsey, Brown Swiss, or Ayrshire) and for meat (e.g., Angus, Hereford, Charolais, or Limousin) places man in a symbiotic activity. Unlike host or prey, a symbiont, even if enslaved, bred, or cultured, accrues some survival benefit; thus, livestock is safe from natural predators, a premium is placed on their health and longevity, and they are bred under controlled conditions.

For the Time Traveller, a comparison between the Morlocks and either flatworms or human farmers is not unsettling, but the equation of Eloi either to unicellular algae or to cattle is so, indeed, because the Traveller perceives an anatomical kinship with them. He finds it difficult to accept the idea that man has descended into a biological relationship, thought to have been the exclusive province of algae, of insects, and of ruminant mammals. He also has difficulty acknowledging the fact that a symbiotic arrangement, even if predacious or parasitic, can benefit its constituents, at least in some measure: the Morlocks gather Eloi like cattle, devour them periodically, but allow for the replenishment of the captive population; the Elois' contentment and biological comfort are, therefore, in the Morlocks' long-range interest as a species. Ironically, outside this mutualistic system, the Eloi are unlikely to survive since they depend upon their captors for food and shelter; thus, for the Eloi, extinction is inescapable without the carnivorous paternalism of the Morlocks. As pastoralists in an ecologically fabricated region, the Morlocks recognize the precariousness of their own situation: if not for the Eloi, they would starve. Each sub-species, therefore, depends upon the other for life, and their interaction is the product of natural selection.

The Time Traveller perceives the fact that the Eloi are indeed "mere fatted cattle, which the ant-like Morlocks preserved and preyed upon— [and] probably saw to the breeding of" (*OTM*.63). But he suspects that their interaction is more than a matter of hunting down and of slaying wild game. As he compares the Morlocks to ants, and as he implies that the Eloi are analogous to ant "cattle" or homopteran insects, he inadvertently acknowledges the symbiotic character of this relationship. The analogy of the flatworm and the algae, he seems to suggest, may not tell us the essential story. In my view, the ant-homopteran analogy is imprecise, for it too-closely correlates the Morlocks to ants, reducing their extraordinary intelligence to nothing more than hard-wired instinct.

To understand the dissimilarity between Morlocks and ants, we can begin by reading *The Science of Life*, in which Wells and his collaborators discuss the evolution of domesticity among species of pastoral ants. They allude, specifically, to three subfamilies of ants, the *Myrmicinae*, the *Dolichoderinae*, and the *Formicinae*, all of which attend to "homopterans," insects such as the aphids and coccids (Wilson 420–3). While some ants devour homopterans or crop their herd (as the Morlocks do to the Eloi), most of the pastoral species keep domestic insects (*SL*.1169). These "ant-cows" (Linnaeus's phrase) furnish the ants with a nutritive liquid, called "honeydew." Since the ant does not have sucking mouth parts (their jaws are designed to bite), they cannot extract plant sap (*SL*.1169). The proboscis of the aphids and of other insects, on the other hand, is designed to extract this liquid from plants which they either drop on leaves or excrete for the ants. In the latter case, the ants "milk" the cows by gently stroking their abdomens for secretions (*SL*.1169); hence, the ant-homopteran association, even though the aphids are the subordinate species, is a mutually beneficial arrangement (Wilson 422–23). *Myrmecophilous* aphids, for instance, have evolved in such a way that their defensive structures such as secretions have been reduced or lost while other anatomical features have developed in such a way as to accommodate the ants. The evidence confirms that the ants' response to homopterans, Edward O. Wilson points out, is so specialized as to represent "an adaptation on their part" (421). The same is true of the Eloi, whose docility and mental inadequacy Wells intended as evolutionary accommodations to the Morlocks.

The most problematic aspect of the Time Traveller's analysis of man's descent in the 800th millennia concerns the nature of the Morlocks who appear to be living contradictions. The most obvious irony is that the Eloi, with whom the Traveller identifies physically, have the mental capacity of five-year-old children (*OTM*.25), whereas the primitive-looking Morlocks are intellectually closer to the Traveller than he dares to admit. How are we to account for the Morlocks' startling characteristics? The concepts of micro-geographic isolation, of mutation, and of natural selection will help us to understand the evolutionary significance of their physical attributes. They have existed in a dark, cold, and inhospitable environment. Through natural selection, favorable mutations permitted some to adapt to the subterranean environment, in the process rendering them uniquely different from their forebears and from their terrestrial relatives, the Eloi. Although these unique traits—photophobia, etiolation, carnivorousness, nocturnality, and hairiness—appear *prima facie* to be primitive or retrogressive, the pertinacity of the Morlocks in this *biotope* evidences the workings of evolutionary biology under adverse conditions. In "Zoological Retrogression" (1891), Wells does not discount the adaptive potential of traits that appear to be regressive: "The zoologist demonstrates that advance has been fitful and uncertain; rapid progress has often been followed by extinction or degeneration, while ... a form lowly and degraded has in its degradation, often happened upon some fortunate discovery or valuable discipline and risen again ... to victory" (*EW*.167–8). Robert M. Philmus describes Wells's idea aptly as "nature's way of doubling back to take a new trail," and thereby adjusting to changing environmental conditions (*EW*.150; [1970] 69–78).

Without the relentless winnowing of natural selection, intensified by geographical isolation, the Morlocks would have wandered blindly in the darkness, starving and freezing to death, until finally becoming extinct. Intermediate forms of Morlocks may have existed, but those unsuited to subterranean life died out: for example, those lacking a heavy coat of hair would have succumbed to the cold; omnivorous or unaggressive ones would have starved to death; and those needing ultraviolet light for vitamin D metabolism would have crumbled in their skins. In effect, these creatures, whom the Time Traveller derogates as throwbacks and whom the Eloi justifiably fear, are the products of evolutionary biology, all that nature would allow in the 800th millennia of geological time.

The Time Traveller certainly acknowledges that the Morlocks are skilled technicians even though he devaluates their actual ability. On the one hand, he rightly assumes that they support the Eloi, making their garments (including metal work), and cultivating their fruit—and all of this in conjunction with having built and maintained an underground city, featuring "an extensive system of subterranean ventilation" (*OTM*.41). As John Huntington rightly asserts, the Morlocks are exemplary technologists who control their environment (46). Compelling evidence of this is the Traveller's discovery of underground power looms: "Huge machines with running belts and whirling fly-wheels … [that] appeared to be weaving machines … worked by leather belts running over drums upon great rotating shafts that stretched across the cavern" (*DTM*.170). Even if the Morlocks inherited these textile systems, and even if they functioned solely as maintenance workers, their mechanical skill is undeniable. The complex technology of an underground ventilation system and of power looms requires great aptitude, especially in the training of new generations of engineers, in the manufacturing of replacement parts, and in the refining of oil for the lubrication of metal parts. The Morlocks, in short, are adept engineers. The Traveller is surprised to find his stolen machine has been "carefully oiled and cleaned," which leads him to suspect "that the Morlocks had … partially taken it to pieces while trying in their dim way to grasp its purpose" (*OTM*.79). If the Morlocks can take complex machinery apart and re-assemble it in working condition, this implies a capacity to communicate, to learn, and, above all, to invent. Most impressive is that, without a plan, they remember where the parts fit in a three-dimensional matrix. It's doubtful that a turn-of-the-century engineer, if presented with the conundrum of the machine, would have been able to do much better than the Morlocks. We must also reflect on the fact that the Morlocks planned and realized an immense capital project in the air vents which were designed to scale as access routes.

Despite all that he has seen, the Time Traveller obstinately denies the civic ingenuity of the Morlocks and is unable to reconcile their archaic anatomy with their mechanical aptitude, textile industry, domestic farming, horticulture, and ecological engineering. He accounts for his affinity to the Eloi in the simplest of terms: "However great their intellectual degradation, the Eloi had kept too much of the human form not to claim my sympathy, and to make me perforce a sharer in their degradation and their Fear" (*OTM*.63). According to a later passage, he accepts the idea of the Morlocks' lineal descent from his own species, which is abundantly clear as he expresses his irrational inclination to kill them: "Very inhuman, you may think, to want to go killing one's own descendants! But it was impossible, somehow, to feel any humanity in the things" (*OTM*.67).

The Time Traveller's discomfort with the idea of man's zoological origins brings to mind Thomas Henry Huxley's opinion on the subject. In "On the Relations of Man to the Lower Animals" (1863), he dismisses the idea that "the belief in the unity of origin of man and brutes involves the brutalization and degradation of the former" (130). I think Huxley would have appreciated the Morlocks and their ironic character. For the Time Traveller, however, the idea of the lineal descent of the Morlocks from twentieth-century humanity contradicts the prevailing anthropological theories to which he obdurately subscribes. Perhaps, as a consequence of his inability to accept his genetic heritage, he must degrade their human intelligence to the level of "habit." Here, he is speaking of "habit" in a primitive, neurological sense—that is, in terms of "ancient and departed necessities" that impress behavior "on the organism" (*OTM*.58). To him, the subterranean species can amount to nothing more than social insects, scurrying out of an "ant-hill" (*OTM*.60). Yet, in the *National Observer*, the Time Traveller is portrayed as an insightful, well-informed naturalist who, while debating his contemporaries, attempts to account for the Morlocks' regressive morphology. He rejects the concept of progressive evolution when he says that, "'In the past ... evolution has not always been upward. The land animals, including ourselves ... are the descendants of almost amphibious mudfish that were hunted out of the seas by the ancestors of the modern sharks'" (*DTM*.173). So the idea of evolutionary regression, even for the highest of all primates, is (in Wells's opinion) neither self-contradictory nor heretical; it may, in fact, be a momentary detour of the evolutionary impulse for mankind. For "the red-haired man," however, even if temporary, the prospect of human descent is perturbing, especially for one who appears resistant to the implications of Darwin's work: for this persona, such a view delimits human existence to "'a little island in time and a little island in space, the surface of the little globe out of all the oceans of space, and a few thousand years out of eternity'" (*DTM*.173).

The most forthright spokesman for evolutionary progressivism in the *National Observer* is "the common-sense person" who propounds a heuristic view of the human species that is not in keeping with the laws of biology. We shall discover that, in the "Atlantic" edition of the novella, the Time Traveller will struggle to reconcile the idealism of "the common-sense person" with his own fundamental knowledge of zoology stemming from Darwin and Huxley. The opposition of these views, which proves to be the source of his theoretical confusion, will interfere with his ability to understand the morphologies of the Eloi and the Morlocks, to determine their relationship to his species, and, finally, to perceive how the two species relate to each other biologically. Consequently, in the anthropological content of his narrative, the Traveller substitutes preconceived judgments for detailed observations and for reasoned deductions.

What accounts for the Traveller's failure or inability to ascribe intellectual acumen to the Morlocks? The most obvious reason for his confusion is a morphological fallacy: the assumption that, since the Eloi are biologically similar to him, a cultural and intellectual kinship must therefore exist between them. By the same token, he assumes that, since the Morlocks do not look like *Homo sapiens sapiens*, they must be debased idiots.

I can identify a culturally ingrained source for the Time Traveller's assumptions about intelligence and morphology. At the turn of the century, the idea that the mental processes of savage man were akin to those of either children or criminals was taken for granted (Stocking 126). Anthropologists of the late Victorian period conjectured that savage man, whether archaic or contemporary, was mentally undeveloped. Since the savage mind in maturity was that of a child and not of a civilized European adult, he reacted to his environment autonomically, instinctively, or irrationally (Stocking 131). Herbert Spencer, in 1895, promulgated the idea of primitive automatism and contributed to the broader view that the "lower" races (those with dark skin) were uncivilized. Civilization, on the other hand, was synonymous with European society (Stocking 131). A number of other prominent scientists contributed to this interpretation of native mentality. Cesare Lombroso (1836–1909), Italian physician and criminologist, compared criminals to animals, to so-called savages, and to people of "lower races" (Gould [1981]:24–27). The late-Victorian fascination with primitivity focusing on Africans and on the urban poor, Carlo Pagetti perceptively observes, has a bearing on *The Time Machine*, because it elucidates the Time Traveller's "moral and psychological reaction to the Morlocks" (130). And Loren Eisley points out that rigid and simplistic assumptions, such as those promulgated by some Victorian naturalists, derived from anthropological paradigms having little to do with the kind of cultural relativism one associates with, and expects from, modern cultural anthropology: "Nineteenth-century social evolutionists had shown a tendency to take the varied non-literate cultures of modern primitives and arrange them in a sort of phylogenetic sequence leading to advanced Western culture. There was little attempt to examine the actual functioning of these communities. They were seen primarily much as … living ancestral social forms, surviving into the present" (340). The bestial appearance of the Morlocks may have evoked a similar categorical reaction from the Time Traveller who faces the intellectual contradiction that the superior civilization in the 800th millennia is comprised of "pallid little monsters" (*DTM*.172), rather than of lightly complexioned pastoralists.

Although the Morlocks are undoubtedly predatory creatures, and although they subjugate the Eloi, they co-exist with them symbiotically. The Morlocks feed, breed, and eat the Eloi, but they preserve the greater population upon which their own species depends for its sustenance. The Eloi, on the other hand, live in an idyllic setting, the ecology of which has been designed to support their basic needs. Apparently unperturbed by their foreshortened life-spans (*DTM*.165), they procreate and luxuriate diurnally. Paradoxically, had the Time Traveller destroyed the Morlock population completely, under the misconceived notion that he was liberating an enslaved people, and had he left the Eloi to their own devices, he would have ensured the latter's very rapid extinction, for they are adapted to the Morlocks' dominion.

Extinction

Three essays preface Wells's vision of extinction in *The Time Machine* (*OTM*.80–5) and illustrate the paradigmatic order of human cultures predominant in nineteenth-century social thought, the implications of which he would criticize as "Excelsior biology" (*EW*.159). In "A Vision of the Past" (June 1887), a future visionary confronts three-eyed "philosophic amphibians," parodies of twentieth-century man. They suffer from intellectual hubris, believing their species to be the pinnacle of human evolution. Whereas the dreamer rightly castigates these creatures, ironically, he suffers from a similar delusion, assuming that these creatures are actually the archaic forerunners of his own higher species; moreover, he claims to be on the line of privileged ascent to a kind of biological apotheosis (*EW*. 159).

Wells supplements this parody with periodical literature on the subject. In the 30 September 1893 essay "On Extinction," which I have already cited, he elucidates several legitimate causes of species extinction, namely climatic changes and the aggression of enemies. The forces to which Wells alludes work inexorably and subtly, and they appear to affect a limited ecological area. Wells stresses that the background forces responsible for the extinction of species in the Jurassic or Cretaceous periods have remained constant. Despite the predominance of mankind in the modern era, secured through transportation technology, geographical discovery, and the species' global diffusion, dynamic changes in the ecology are unrelentingly active and (the implication is) mankind is not above them. He cites the bison, the seal, and the Greenland whale as instances of extinction: "It is not only the dodo that has gone; for dozens of genera and hundreds of species, this century has witnessed the writing on the wall" (*EW*.170). His earliest work in science, in fact, coincides with the contemporaneous extinction of the Great Auk (mid 1800s), the American Heath hen (1870), the South African quagga (a zebra) (1883), and the Portuguese ibex (1892) (Lassem 106–7); overgrazing and overhunting probably caused these events to occur, and mankind was at fault in each case.

In a second piece, "The Extinction of Man," Wells considers the prospect of human extinction. Although "the days of man's triumph" are at hand, this tenure represents a mere moment in geological time (*EW*.171). Nor does man's primacy confer immunity to pandemic disease (172). The fossil record, which has never shown "a really dominant species succeeded by its own descendants," is a reliable predictor of the future of mankind. It is entirely conceivable, Wells suggests, that plague bacilli, ants, or crustaceans may outlast the human species (*EW*.205–6).

In the imaginative frontiers of *The Time Machine*, Wells encounters the extinction of man, and it is to this end that the novel invariably points. He sent a copy to T. H. Huxley, in May 1895, identifying *The Time Machine* as a testing ground for biological theory. As David C. Smith observes, the novel becomes the context within which the possibilities, as well as the probabilities, of human evolution are worked out (98).

13

The Paleoanthropologist
as Literary Critic

This study has been largely concerned with the ways in which imaginative writers use paleoanthropology in their fictional works. As a postscript, I would like to consider how paleoanthropologists use imaginative literature in their writings.

In technical scientific works, literary allusions tend to be adornments at best. But, in works geared to broader audiences, one finds tangential allusions to great writers and familiar quotes that are used for comparative insight into a scientific area of concern. Bernard G. Campbell's excellent undergraduate text, *Humankind Emerging*, contains references to Balzac, Longfellow, Shakespeare, Shelley, and H. G. Wells. Of these seven textual references, most are epigraphic, comprising a quote that reflects a chapter theme. But, on several occasions, Campbell incorporates a writer's discourse directly into his own text to enhance his discussion of the scientific material. Balzac's enthusiastic appreciation of Cuvier's paleontological reconstructions, for example, enhances Campbell's survey of the pioneers of paleoanthropology. The respected opinion of Balzac in this context is important, since the focus of Campbell's writing is the historical culture within which early natural historians worked. As I have shown in the cases of Verne and Burroughs, the cultural ethos can influence the way scientific information is disseminated. Generally, I think it valid to say that literary allusions in anthropological contexts elucidate scientific content. Many scientific writers realize full well that the study of man is a broad cultural endeavor, validly expressed in many forms of discourse.

I would like to close with an interesting example of how anthropologists can express varying degrees of critical sensibility in their readings of fiction. The piece in question is one that we have worked on closely: Wells's "The Grisly Folk." And I would like to compare the critical evaluations of this story in three texts: Bernard G. Campbell's *Humankind Emerging*, Christopher Stringer and Robin McKie's *African Exodus*, and Milford Wolpoff and Rachel Caspari's *Race and Human Evolution*. The question I am asking is as follows: can a scientist's critical appreciation of imaginative literature assist in the understanding and communication of knowledge about prehistoric humanity?

Campbell's opinion, which is a point of reference for the other critiques, is that Wells distorted the image of the Neanderthal, and that this distortion owed its genesis to Marcellin Boule's skeletal misconstruction. Because Campbell believes that imaginative literature and scientific discovery are intimately related to one another, and that each, in turn, can be influenced by political, philosophical and cultural ideas, Wells's work (as much as Boule's or the opinion of the anatomist Elliot Smith) appears to be, in his view, an index of its intellectual climate.

Stringer and McKie's literary criticism, however, does not follow Campbell's example directly. They agree with the latter's assessment of the Neanderthal's public image having been unjustifiably degraded in the literature because of Boule's errors, and because of deep-seated anti-Germanic feelings after World War I (15). But, from this point on, I believe that these authors do not read the imaginative literature carefully enough. I agree with their statement that fictional writers such as Wells use the Neanderthal stereotype, but I disagree with the particular charge that J.-H. Rosny-Aîné (whose name is unfortunately misprinted: "J. L. Rosny-Aine*s*") is guilty in this regard. They cite the following passage as evidence that Rosny follows Wells in the disparaging portrayal of the Neanderthals: "Nothing of his face was visible but a mouth bordered by raw flesh and a pair of murderous eyes. His squat stature exaggerated the length of his arms and the enormous width of his shoulders. His whole being expressed a brutal strength, tireless and without pity" (15–16). First of all, Stringer and McKie's identification of the Oulhamrs as Neanderthals is highly questionable. A closer reading of the text against its anthropological background suggests that the tribe in question (as I have shown) more likely consists of *erecti*. Furthermore, the personae in question, Aghoo and his brothers, are Naoh's rivals in the quest for fire. Rather than being stereotyped Neanderthals, as Stringer and McKie believe, they are actually misanthropic *erecti* whose bad temperament dramatically contrasts with the devotion and camaraderie of Naoh's tribe. The most important point to keep in mind is that they are likely not Neanderthals (16).

In addition to the misprint and the misidentification, Stringer and McKie wrongly contend that Golding's *The Inheritors* successfully rehabilitates the image of the Neanderthal. Quite the opposite is true, as I have indicated. Despite Golding's deliberate effort to malign the Cro-Magnons and to favor the Neanderthals, the latter is endowed with a consciousness that derives from Boule's misconstruction and craniometric theory. Rehabilitation is Golding's intention, but his efforts are unsuccessful because they rely on unauthorized science. In view of these two points, I believe that Stringer and McKie fail to enlist the fiction as an informative resource in their book.

Wolpoff and Caspari, elaborating on Stringer and McKie's idea of the Neanderthals as a vilified minority, reveal their understanding of the idea of the alien in science fiction. They use the literature perceptively to describe the moral effects of alienation and of segregation. For Wolpoff and Caspari, the Neanderthals have become for us what native people once were: that is, the "other" or alien counterpart to the modern selfhood (276–77). But their presence in the literature also allows us to define ourselves; thus, the literary image of prehistoric humanity is mimetic. Wells presents the Neanderthals as impersonal and grotesque beings with mask-like faces, great brow ridges, and no forehead—features that rob them of human personality. Wolpoff and Caspari realize, however, that Golding is complicit in this practice: he, too, distorts the Neanderthals' physiognomy, accentuating their flaring nostrils, their lack of a nasal bridge, and their jutting jaw (which actually receded). Other works, they allege, fall into this category. For example, Isaac Asimov's short story "The Ugly Little Boy" depicts a Neanderthal boy as ugly and misshapen, while Jean Auel's hominids have an exaggerated snout, a low forehead, and beak-like nose (although, on this score, I defend Auel's accuracy). Although the stereotyped ugliness of the Neanderthal man has remained unchanged for over eighty years, the authors maintain that their behavior has undergone some modification in the fiction. The mindless brute in Wells's story has become an articulate and sympathetic persona in Asimov's story, while Auel's hominids are culturally sophisticated and endearing. I concur with these authors' claim that fictive Neanderthals function "like the natives whose roles they inherited by becoming the 'other.'" I think this contention is persuasively borne out in Lester Del Rey's "The Day Is Done." Wolpoff and Caspari conclude that the fictive Neanderthal provides clear insight into our own identities (276–7). The negative stereotype of the Neanderthal, in my view, reflects a warped cultural viewpoint and serious misconceptions about human prehistory.

Of the three critical readings of the fictive Neanderthal, that of

Wolpoff and Caspari is the most accurate and useful. The difference between the readings of Stringer and McKie, on the one hand, and of Wolpoff and Caspari, on the other, is a matter of emphasis and of care: Stringer and McKie seem to undervalue the imaginative dimension of anthropology as an asset to their discourse, while Wolpoff and Caspari enlist the literature to their advantage and do not treat it as ancillary material; for them, the novel is not a mere novelty.

Generally, the anthropologists I consult here agree that the imaginative literature is, to some degree, an index of larger cultural trends pertaining to the Neanderthals and to other prehistoric beings, and that the literature is more than a superficial indicator of cultural trends. For, as Wolpoff and Caspari show, it functions on a deeper, psychosocial level, as a means of understanding our evolutionary ancestry.

Scientists can benefit from imaginative literature as they assess the historical significance of ancestral humanity. For one, they can identify and redress popular misconceptions, the consequences of pseudo-science and of errant or of obsolete theories. Criticism of this information can have a constructive, edifying purpose if incorrect depictions of prehistoric humanity are understood in their historical and ideological contexts. Imaginative literature that is insightful or anticipatory can augment anthropological discourse and make scientific theory more accessible to the general reader. Read from literary, historical, and scientific perspectives together, prehistoric fiction contributes greatly to our understanding of the human past.

Works Cited

Alles, Gregory D. "Dynamism." Vol. 2 of *The Encyclopedia of Religion*. Ed. Mircea Eliade et al. 15 vols. London: Collier Macmillan; New York: Macmillan, 1987. 526–32.

Allot, Kenneth. *Jules Verne*. London: Cresset, 1940.

Alterman, Peter S. "Aliens in Golding's *The Inheritors*." *Science Fiction Studies* 5.1 (March 1978): 3–10.

Andrews, Peter. "Homininae." *Encyclopedia of Human Evolution and Prehistory*. Ed. Ian Tattersall, Eric Delson, and John Van Couvering. New York: Garland, 247–248.

_____. "Hominoidea." *Encyclopedia of Human Evolution and Prehistory*. 248–55.

Angenot, Marc, and Nadia Khouri. "An International Bibliography of Prehistoric Fiction." *Science Fiction Studies* 8.1 (March 1981): 38–53.

Ardrey, Robert. *African Genesis: A Personal Investigation into the Animal Origins and Nature of Man*. New York: Atheneum, 1970.

Auel, Jean M. *The Clan of the Cave Bear*. New York: Bantam, 1980.

Baker, James R. *William Golding: A Critical Study*. New York: St. Martin's, 1965.

Bolle, Kees W. "Animism and Animitism." Vol. 1 of *The Encyclopedia of Religion*. 296–302.

Bonwick, John. *Daily Life and Origin of the Tasmanians*. Reprint. New York: Johnson Reprint, 1967.

_____. *The Last of the Tasmanians; or, the Black War of Van Diemen's Land*. Reprint. Adelaide, Australia: Libraries Board of South Australia, 1969.

_____. *The Lost Tasmanian Race*. New York: Johnson Reprint, 1970.

Boonzaier, Emile; Penny Berens, Candy Malherbe, and Andy Smith. *The Cape Herders: A History of the Khoikhoi of Southern Africa*. Cape Town & Johannesburg: David Philip; Athens, OH: Ohio University Press, 1996.

Boulle, Pierre. *The Planet of the Apes*. Trans. Xan Fielding. New York: Gramercy Books, 1963.

Brain, C. K. "The Transvaal Ape-Man-Bearing Cave Deposits." *Transvaal Museum Memoir*. No. 11, 1958.

Brandon, S. G. F. "Religion, Origins of." Vol. IV: 92–99 of the *Dictionary of the History of Ideas: Studies of Selected Pivotal Ideas*. Ed. Philip P. Wiener. 4 vols. New York: Scribner's, 1973.

Burroughs, Edgar Rice. *The Land That Time Forgot*. Intro. Mike Resnick. 1924. Rpt. Lincoln: University of Nebraska Press, 1999.

Calder, J. E. *Some Account of the Wars, Extirpation, Habits, etc. of the Native Tribes of Tasmania*. Reprint. Hobart, Tasmania, Australia: Fullers Bookshop, 1972.

Campbell, Bernard G., ed. *Humankind Emerging*. Boston: Little, Brown, 1976.

Camper, Petrus. *Works on the Connexion between the Science of Anatomy and the Arts of Drawing, Painting, Statuary*. In *Readings in Early Anthropology*. Ed. J. S. Slotkin. Viking Fund Publications in Anthropology. No. 40 Gen. Editor Sol Tax. Chicago: Aldine, 1965. 198.

Carlyon, Richard. *A Guide to the Gods: An Essential Guide to World Mythology*. New York: William Morrow, 1981.

Clarke, Arthur C. *2001: A Space Odyssey*. New York: Penguin, 1993.

Clute, John, and Peter Nicholls. "Apes and Cavemen (In the Modern World)." *Encyclopedia of Science Fiction*. New York: St. Martin's, 1995. 46–8.

Corballis, Michael C. *The Lopsided Ape: Evolution of the Generative Mind*. New York: Oxford University Press, 1991.

Costello, Peter. *Jules Verne: Inventor of Science Fiction*. London: Hodder and Stoughton, 1978.

Dart, Raymond. "The First South African Manlike Ape" (1925). In *Man's Discovery of His Past: Literary Landmarks in Archaeology*. Ed. Robert Heizer. Englewood Cliffs, NJ: Prentice-Hall, 1962. 140–48.

_____. "The Predatory Transition from Ape to Man." *International Anthropological and Linguistic Review*. 1 (1954): 207–8.

Dart, Raymond A., with Dennis Craig. *Adventures with the Missing Link*. New York: Harper & Brothers, 1959.

Darwin, Charles. *The Autobiography: 1809–1882*. Ed. Nora Barlow. New York: W. W. Norton, 1958.

_____. *The Descent of Man*. Intro. H. James Birx. 1871. Rpt. Amherst, NY: Prometheus Books, 1998.

_____. "The Essay of 1844." *The Foundations of the Origin of Species: Two Essays Written in 1842 and 1844*. Ed. Francis Darwin. Cambridge: Cambridge University Press, 1909; New York: Kraus Reprint Co., 1969.

_____. *The Origin of Species and The Descent of Man*. 6th ed. New York: Modern Library, 1872.

_____. *The Voyage of the Beagle*. Intro. Walter Sullivan. New York: Meridian, 1996.

Davies, David Michael. *The Last of the Tasmanians*. New York: Barnes & Noble, 1974.

Davies, Nigel. *Human Sacrifice in History and Today*. New York: William Morrow, 1981.

Del Rey, Lester. "The Day Is Done." *The Best of Lester Del Rey*. Intro. Terry Brooks. 1939. New York: Ballantine, 1978. 12–24.

Delson, Eric. "Paleoanthropology." *Encyclopedia of Human Evolution and Prehistory*. 407.

_____, and Ian Tattersall. "Primates." *Encyclopedia of Human Evolution and Prehistory*. 481–84.

De Paolo, Charles. "Wells, Golding, and Auel: Representing the Neanderthal." *Science Fiction Studies* 27.3 (November 2000): 418–38.

De Perthes, Boucher. "On Antédiluvian Man and His Works." In *Man's Discovery of His Past*. 83–93.

Desmond, Adrian. *Huxley: From Devil's Disciple to Evolution's High Priest*. Reading, MA: Addison-Wesley, 1997.

Dobzhansky, Theodosius, et al. *Evolution*. San Francisco: W. H. Freeman, 1977.

Dubois, Eugène. "On Pithecanthropus Erectus: A Transitional Form between Man and the Apes." In *Man's Discovery of His Past*. 126–40.

Durant, Will. *Our Oriental Heritage.* Vol. 1 of *The Story of Civilization.* By Will and Ariel Durant. 11 vols. New York: Simon and Schuster, 1954.

Eisenstein, Alex. *"The Time Machine* and the End of Man." *Science Fiction Studies* 3.2 (July 1976): 161–65.

Eisley, Loren. *Darwin's Century: Evolution and the Men Who Discovered It.* Garden City, NY: Anchor, 1961.

———. "Epilogue: Jack London, Evolutionist." 1962. Rpt. In *Before Adam.* By Jack London. Intro. Dennis L. McKiernan. Lincoln: University of Nebraska Press, 2000. 243–51.

Elliott, H. Chandler. *The Shape of Intelligence: The Evolution of the Human Brain.* New York: Scribner's, 1969.

Evans, Arthur B. *Jules Verne Rediscovered.* New York: Greenwood, 1988.

———. "Science Fiction vs. Scientific Fiction in France: From Jules Verne to J.-H. Rosny Aîné." *Science Fiction Studies* 44 15.1 (March 1988): 1–11; Abstract. http://www.uiowa.edu/__sfs/a44.htm.

———, and Ron Miller. "Jules Verne, Misunderstood Visionary." *Scientific American* (April 1997): http;//www.sciam.com, 1–13.

Finger, Stanley. *Origins of Neuroscience: A History of Explorations into Brain Function.* New York: Oxford University Press, 1994.

Formigari, Lia. "The Great Chain of Being." Vol. I: 325–35 of *Dictionary of the History of Ideas: Studies of Selected Pivotal Ideas.*

Frazer, Sir James George. *The Golden Bough.* Vol. I (Abridged). New York: Macmillan, 1951.

Freud, Sigmund. *Civilization and Its Discontents.* Ed. and Trans. James Strachey. Intro. Peter Gay. New York: W. W. Norton, 1961.

Golding, William. "Egypt from My Inside." *The Hot Gates and other Occasional Pieces.* New York: Harcourt, 1965. 71–82.

———. *The Inheritors.* New York: Harcourt, 1955.

Gould, Stephen Jay. *Eight Little Piggies: Reflections in Natural History.* New York: W. W. Norton, 1993.

———. *Ever Since Darwin: Reflections in Natural History.* New York: W. W. Norton, 1977.

———. *The Mismeasure of Man.* New York: W. W. Norton, 1981.

———. *The Panda's Thumb: More Reflections in Natural History.* New York: W. W. Norton, 1980.

Grant, Michael. *Myths of the Greeks and Romans.* New York: Mentor, 1962.

Grine, Fred E. "Australopithecus." *Encyclopedia of Human Evolution and Prehistory.* 67–74.

———. "Makapansgat." *Encyclopedia of Human Evolution and Prehistory.* 329–30.

Haeckel, Ernst. *The Riddle of the Universe.* Trans. Joseph McCabe. Ed. H. James Birx. Buffalo, NY: Prometheus Books, 1992.

Harrelson, Walter J. "Ten Commandments." *The Interpreter's Dictionary of the Bible: An Illustrated Encyclopedia.* Ed. George Arthur Buttrick et al. 5 vols. 1962. Nashville: Abingdon, 1993. Vol. 4, R-Z: 569–73.

Hartland, E. Sidney. "Totemism." Vol. XII: Suffering-Zwingli: 393–407. *Encyclopedia of Religion and Ethics.* James Hastings et al. New York: Scribner's, n.d.

Haynes, Roslynn D. *H. G. Wells: Discoverer of the Future; The Influence of Science on His Work.* New York: New York University Press, 1980.

Hays, H. R. *From Ape to Angel: An Informal History of Social Anthropology.* New York: Capricorn, 1964.

Heizer, Robert F., ed. *Man's Discovery of His Past; Literary Landmarks in Archaeology.* Trans. Stephen Heizer. Englewood Cliffs, NJ: Prentice-Hall, 1962.

Hempel, Johannes. "Psalms, Book of." *The Interpreter's Dictionary of the Bible*. Vol. 3, K-Q: 942–58.

Herodotus. *The Histories*. Trans. Aubrey de Sélincourt. Rev. and Intro. A. R. Burns. Harmondsworth: Penguin, 1972.

Himmelfarb, Gertrude. *Darwin and the Darwinian Revolution*. New York: W. W. Norton, 1962.

Holloway, Ralph L. "*Brain*." *Encyclopedia of Human Evolution and Prehistory*. 98–105.

Hrdlička, Arles. "The Most Ancient Skeletal Remains of Man (1913)." *Source Book in Anthropology*. Ed. A. L. Kroeber and T. T. Waterman. *Landmarks in Anthropology*. Gen. Ed. Weston La Barre. 1931. Rev. ed. New York: Harcourt, 1965. 43–67.

Huntington, John. *The Logic of Fantasy: H. G. Wells and Science Fiction*. New York: Columbia University Press, 1982.

Huxley, Thomas Henry. "On the Fossil Remains of Man." *Evidence as to Man's Place in Nature*. New York: Appleton, 1863. 139–84.

_____. "On the Relations of Man to the Lower Animals." *Evidence as to Man's Place in Nature*. 71–132.

Jastrow, Robert. *The Enchanted Loom: Mind in the Universe*. New York: Simon & Schuster, 1981.

Johanson, Donald, and Maitland Edey. *Lucy: The Beginnings of Humankind*. New York: Warner Books, 1981.

Kay, Richard F. "Teeth." *Encyclopedia of Human Evolution and Prehistory*. 571–78.

Keith, Sir Arthur. "Faith in Piltdown Man." In *The World of the Past*. Ed. Jacquetta Hawkes. 3 vols. New York: Alfred A. Knopf, 1971. I. 210–13.

Kerr, Robert. *Psychomotor Learning*. New York: Holt, 1982.

Ketterer, David. "Oedipus as Time Traveller." *Science Fiction Studies* 9.3 (November 1982): 340–1.

Kinkead-Weekes, Mark and Ian Gregor. *William Golding: A Critical Study*. New York: Harcourt, 1967.

Kneale, Matthew. *English Passengers*. New York: Anchor, 2001.

Krumm, Pascale. "*The Island of Doctor Moreau*, or the Case of Devolution." *Foundation: The International Review of Science Fiction* 28.75 (Spring 1999): 51–62.

Kuhn, Thomas S. *The Structure of Scientific Revolutions*. Foundation of the Unity of Science. International Encyclopedia of Unified Science. Vol. II. 2nd ed. Chicago: University of Chicago Press, 1970.

Kunzig, Robert. "Learning to Love Neanderthal." *Discover*. 20.8 August 1999: 68–75.

Laitman, Jeffrey T. "The Anatomy of Human Speech." *Natural History* 93 (1984): 20–7.

_____. "Speech (Origins of)." *Encyclopedia of Human Evolution and Prehistory*. 539–40.

Lassem, Don. *Dinosaurs to Dodos: An Encyclopedia of Extinct Animals*. New York: Scholastic, 1999.

Leakey, Richard, and Roger Lewin. *Origins: The Emergence and Evolution of Our Species and Its Possible Future*. New York: Dutton, 1977.

_____, and _____. *Origins Reconsidered: In Search of What Makes Us Human*. New York: Doubleday, 1992.

Lieberman, Philip. *The Biology and Evolution of Language*. Cambridge, MA: Harvard University Press, 1984.

Lima, Mesquitela. "Fetishism." Trans. Monica Varese Andrada. Vol. 5 of *The Encyclopedia of Religion*. 314–17.

Lorenz, Konrad. *On Aggression*. Trans. Marjorie Kerr Wilson. New York: Harcourt, Brace & World, 1966.

Lottman, Herbert R. *Jules Verne: An Exploratory Biography*. New York: St. Martin's, 1996.

Lovejoy, Arthur O. *The Great Chain of Being: A Study of the History of an Idea*. New York: Harper & Row, 1936.

Lynch, Lawrence. *Jules Verne*. New York: Twayne Publishers, 1992.

Mason, Carol; Martin Harry Greenberg, and Patricia Warrick, ed. *Anthropology Through Science Fiction*. New York: St. Martin's, 1974.

Mayr, Ernst. *Animal Species and Evolution*. Cambridge, MA: Harvard University Press, 1965.

_____. *The Growth of Biological Thought: Diversity, Evolution, and Inheritance*. Cambridge, MA: Harvard University Press, 1982.

_____. "The Taxonomic Evaluation of Fossil Hominids." In *Classification and Human Evolution*. Ed. Sherwood L. Washburn. Chicago: Aldine, 1963. 332–46.

Messadié, Gerald. *Great Scientific Discoveries*. Chambers Encyclopedic Guides. Edinburgh: Chambers, 1991.

Montagu, Ashley. *Man: His First Two Million Years; A Brief Introduction to Anthropology*. New York: Dell, 1968.

_____. *The Nature of Human Aggression*. New York: Oxford University Press, 1976.

Morris, Desmond. *The Naked Ape: A Zoologist's Study of the Human Animal*. 1967. New York: Delta, 1999.

Mullen, Richard Dale. "An Annotated Survey of Books and Pamphlets by H. G. Wells." *H. G. Wells and Modern Science Fiction*. Ed. Robert M. Philmus and David Y. Hughes. Lewisburg, PA: Bucknell University Press, 1977. 223–267.

Myers, Bernard S. *Art and Civilization*. New York: McGraw-Hill, 1967.

Oldsey, Bernard S., and Stanley Weintraub. *The Art of William Golding*. New York: Harcourt, 1965.

Ovid (Publius Ovidius Naso). *Metamorphoses*. Trans. A. D. Melville. New York: Oxford University Press, 1986.

Pagetti, Carlo. "Change in the City: The Time Traveller's London and the 'Baseless Fabric' of His Vision." In *H. G. Wells's Perennial Time Machine: Selected Essays from the Centenary Conference, "Time Machine: Past, Present, and Future."* Imperial College, London, July 26–29, Ed. George Slusser, Patrick Parrinder, and Danièle Chatelain. Athens: University of Georgia Press, 2001. 122–34.

Philmus, Robert M. *Into the Unknown: The Evolution of Science Fiction from Francis Godwin to H. G. Wells*. Berkeley University of California Press, 1970.

_____. "The Satiric Ambivalence of *The Island of Doctor Moreau*." *Science Fiction Studies* 8.1 (March 1981): 2–11.

Pilbeam, David. *The Ascent of Man: An Introduction to Human Evolution*. The Macmillan Series in Physical Anthropology. Ed. Elwyn L. Simons and David Pilbeam. New York: Macmillan, 1972.

Popper, Karl R. "Conjectures and Refutations." *Science: Men, Methods, Goals; A Reader: Methods of Physical Science*. Ed. Boruch A. Brody and Nicholas Capaldi. New York: W. A. Benjamin, 1968.

Potts, Richard. "Acheulian." *Encyclopedia of Human Evolution and Prehistory*. 3–6.

Price, A. Grenfell, editor. *The Explorations of Captain James Cook in the Pacific, As Told by Selections of His Own Journals, 1768–1779*. Intro. Percy G. Adams. New York: Dover, 1971.

Prince, John S. "The 'True Riddle of the Sphinx' in *The Time Machine*." *Science Fiction Studies* 27.3 (November 2000): 543–6.

Reader, John. *Missing Links: The Hunt for Earliest Man*. Boston: Little, Brown, 1981.

Redpath, Philip. "Doorways Through Wells: *Lord of the Flies* and *The Inheritors*. In *William Golding's Lord of the Flies*. Ed. and Intro. Harold Bloom. Modern Critical Interpretations. Philadelphia: Chelsea House, 1999. 133–51.

Reed, John R. "H. G. Wells's Familiar Aliens." In *Aliens: The Anthropology of Science Fiction*. Ed. George E. Slusser and Eric S. Rabkin. Alternatives. Gen. ed. Eric S. Rabkin, Martin H. Greenberg, & Joseph D. Olander. Carbondale: Southern Illinois University Press, 1987. 145–56.

_____. *The Natural History of H. G. Wells*. Athens: Ohio University Press, 1982.

Reilly, Patrick. "*Lord of the Flies*: Beelzebub's Boys." In *William Golding's Lord of the Flies*. 169–90.

Retzius, Gustav. "The Development of Race Measurements and Classification" (Huxley Lecture for 1909). In *Source Book in Anthropology*. 94–102.

Rightmire, Philip H. "Homo Erectus." *Encyclopedia of Human Evolution and Prehistory*. 259–65.

Roberts, Ian F. "Maupertuis: Doppelgänger of Doctor Moreau." *Science Fiction Studies* 28.2 (July 2001): 261–74.

Rosenberger, Alfred L. "Anthropoidea." *Encyclopedia of Human Evolution and Prehistory*. 31–8.

_____. "Scala Naturae." *Encyclopedia of Human Evolution and Prehistory*. 504.

Rosny-Aîné, J.-H. (pseudonym, Joseph-Henri Boëx). *Quest for Fire*. Trans. Harold Talbott. 1911. Harmondsworth, UK: Penguin, 1982.

Rostand, J. "General Biology." In the *History of Science: The Beginnings of Modern Science from 1450 to 1800*. Ed. René Taton. Trans. A. J. Pomerans. New York: Basic Books, 1964. 511–26.

Rudgley, Richard. *The Lost Civilizations of the Stone Age*. New York: Free Press, 1999.

Scafella, Frank. "The White Sphinx and *The Time Machine*." *Science Fiction Studies* 8.3 (November 1981): 255–65.

Schaaffhausen, D. "On the Crania of the Most Ancient Races of Man." 1858. Rpt. as "Discovery of the Neanderthal Skull." In *Man's Discovery of His Past*. 116–23.

Schwartz, Jeffrey H. *The Red Ape: Orang-utans and Human Origins*. Boston: Houghton-Mifflin, 1987.

Serafini, Anthony. *The Epic History of Biology*. New York: Plenum, 1993.

Shipman, Pat. *The Man Who Found the Missing Link: Eugène Dubois and His Lifelong Quest to Prove Darwin Right*. New York: Simon and Schuster, 2001.

_____. "The Myths and Perturbing Realities of Cannibalism." *Discover* (March 1987): 70–6.

Shirer, William L. *The Rise and Fall of the Third Reich: A History of Nazi Germany*. New York: Simon and Schuster, 1960.

Shreeve, James. *The Neanderthal Enigma: Solving the Mystery of Modern Human Origins*. New York: Morrow, 1995.

Slotkin, J. S., ed. *Readings in Early Anthropology*. No. 40 of the Viking Fund Publications in Anthropology. Ed. Sol Tax. Chicago: Aldine, 1965.

Smith, David C. *H. G. Wells, Desperately Mortal: A Biography*. New Haven: Yale University Press, 1986.

Soffer-Bobyshev, Olga. "Bordes, François (1919–1981)." *Encyclopedia of Human Evolution and Prehistory*. 97.

Spencer, Frank. "Boule, [Pierre] Marcellin (1861–1942)." *Encyclopedia of Human Evolution and Prehistory*. 97.

_____. "Dart, Raymond Arthur (b. 1893)." *Encyclopedia of Human Evolution and Prehistory*. 152.

_____. "Piltdown." *Encyclopedia of Human Evolution and Prehistory*. 452–53.

_____. "Virchow, Rudolph (1821–1902)." *Encyclopedia of Human Evolution and Prehistory*. 595.

_____. "Von Koenigswald, Gustav H. Ralph (1902–1982)." *Encyclopedia of Human Evolution and Prehistory*. 298.

_____. "Woodward, [Sir] Arthur Smith (1864–1944)." *Encyclopedia of Human Evolution and Prehistory*. 599.

Stableford, Brian. "Origin of Man." *The Encyclopedia of Science Fiction*. 894–5.

Stocking, George W. "The Dark-Skinned Savage: The Image of Primitive Man in Evolutionary Anthropology." In *Race, Culture, and Evolution: Essays in the History of Anthropology*. By George W. Stocking. New York: Free Press, 1968. 110–32.

Storr, Anthony. *Human Aggression*. New York: Bantam, 1968.

Stover, Leon E. "Afterword." *Apeman, Spaceman: Anthropological Science Fiction*. Ed. Leon Stover and Harry Harrison. Foreword Carleton S. Coon. Garden City, NY: Doubleday, 1968. 311–51.

_____, ed. *The Time Machine: An Invention: A Critical Text of the 1895 London First Edition, with an Introduction and Appendices*. Ed. Leon Stover. Jefferson, NC: McFarland, 1986.

Strauss, William L., Jr. "The Great Piltdown hoax." *Anthropology*. Ed. Samuel Rapport and Helen Wright. New York University Library of Science. Editorial Adviser, Joseph Bram. New York: New York University Press, 1969. 45–55.

Stringer, Christopher B. "Boule [Pierre] Marcellin (1861–1972." *Encyclopedia of Human Evolution and Prehistory*. 97.

_____. "The Emergence of Modern Humans." *Scientific American* 26.6 (1990): 68–74.

_____. "Gibraltar." *Encyclopedia of Human Evolution and Prehistory*. 225.

_____. "Homo Sapiens." *Encyclopedia of Human Evolution and Prehistory*. 267–74.

_____. "Neanderthals." *Encyclopedia of Human Evolution and Prehistory*. 366–72.

_____. "Skhūl." *Encyclopedia of Human Evolution and Prehistory*. 523.

_____. "Spy." *Encyclopedia of Human Evolution and Prehistory*. 540.

_____, and Robin McKie. *African Exodus: The Origins of Modern Humanity*. New York: Holt, 1996.

"Symbiosis." *Concise Encyclopedia: Biology*. Trans. and Revised Thomas A. Scott. Berlin: Walter de Gruyter, 1996.

Tattersall, Ian. "Classification." *Encyclopedia of Human Evolution and Prehistory*. 136–38.

_____. *The Human Odyssey: Four Million Years of Human Evolution*. New York: Prentice-Hall, 1993.

_____. "Systematics." *Encyclopedia of Human Evolution and Prehistory*. 558–59.

Toth, Nick, and Kathy Schick. "Fire." *Encyclopedia of Human Evolution and Prehistory*. 207–8.

_____. "Paleolithic Lifeways." *Encyclopedia of Human Evolution and Prehistory*. 429–35.

_____. "Stone-Tool Making." *Encyclopedia of Human Evolution and Prehistory*. 542–48.

Travers, Robert. *The Tasmanians; the Story of a Doomed Race*. Melbourne, Australia: Cassel, 1968.

Tylor, Edward Burnett. *Primitive Culture*. London: John Murray, 1871. 1–25. Rpt. in *Readings in Anthropology*. 2nd ed. Ed. Morton H. Fried. New York: Thomas Y. Crowell, 1968. II: 1–18.

Urry, J. "Headhunters and Body-snatchers." *Anthropology Today* 5.5 (1989): 11–13.

Verne, Jules. *The Village in the Treetops*. Trans. I. O. Evans. 1901. Westport, CT: Associated Booksellers, 1964.

Vernier, J. P. "The Science Fiction of J. H. Rosny the Elder." *Science Fiction Studies* 2.2 (July 1975): 156–63.

Villiers, Allan. *Captain James Cook*. New York: Scribner's, 1967.

Wallace, Alfred Russel. "On the Tendency of Varieties to Depart Indefinitely from the Original Type." In *Charles Darwin: The Development of the Theory of Natural Selection*. Ed. and Intro. Thomas F. Glick and David Kohn. Indianapolis: Hackett, 1996. 337–345.

Wardhaugh, Ronald. *Introduction to Linguistics*. New York: McGraw-Hill, 1972.

Weiner, J. S. "The Piltdown Affair." In *The World of the Past*. Vol. 1: 213–29.

_____, K. P. Oakley, and W. E. Le Gros Clark. "The Solution of the Piltdown Problem." In *Man's Discovery of His Past*. 30–6.

Wells, H. G. *The Complete Short Stories*. Ed. John Hammond. London: J. M. Dent, 1998.

_____. *The Conclusion of a Short History of the World*. Revised edition. In *The Last Books of H. G. Wells: The Happy Turning and Mind at the End of Its Tether*. Ed. and Intro. G. P. Wells. Baskerville: H. G. Wells Society, 1982.

_____. *The Correspondence*. Ed. David C. Smith. 4 vols. London: Pickering, 1996.

_____. *Early Writings in Science and Science Fiction*. By H. G. Wells. Ed. Robert M. Philmus and David Y. Hughes. Berkeley: University of California Press, 1975.

_____. *Experiment in Autobiography: Discoveries and Conclusions of a Very Ordinary Brain (Since 1866)*. New York: Macmillan, 1934.

_____. "The Grisly Folk." *H. G. Wells: Selected Short Stories*. London: Penguin, 1979. 285–98.

_____. "Human Evolution as an Artificial Process." Appendix 5. *The Island of Doctor Moreau: A Variorum Text*. Ed. Robert M. Philmus. Athens: University of Georgia Press, 1993.

_____. "Jimmy Goggles the God." *The Country of the Blind and Other Stories*. Ed. and Intro. Michael Sherborne. New York: Oxford University Press, 1996. 286–99.

_____. "The Lord of the Dynamos." *The Country of the Blind and Other Stories*. 75–84.

_____. "*The National Observer Time Machine*." Appendix III of *The Definitive Time Machine: A Critical Edition of H. G. Wells's Scientific Romance*. Intro. and notes Harry M. Geduld. Bloomington: Indiana University Press, 1987.

_____. *The Outline of History, Being a Plain History of Life and Mankind*. Revised by Raymond Postgate, 2 vols. 1920. Rpt. Garden City, NY: Doubleday, 1949.

_____. "A Story of the Stone Age." *Twenty-Eight Science Fiction Stories of H. G. Wells*. Ed. Groff Conklin. New York: Dover, 1952. 316–417.

_____. *Textbook of Biology*. London: W. B. Clive & Co., 1892.

_____. *The Time Machine* (Atlantic Edition). *H. G. Wells: The Time Machine and The Island of Doctor Moreau*. Ed. and Intro. Patrick Parrinder. New York: Oxford University Press, 1996.

_____. *The War of the Worlds: A Critical Text of the 1898 First Edition, with an Introduction, Illustrations, and Appendices*. Ed. Leon Stover. Annotated H. G. Wells, vol. 4. Jefferson, NC: McFarland, 2001.

_____, Julian S. Huxley, and G. P. Wells. *The Science of Life*. 4 vols. Garden City, NY: Doubleday, 1929. Rpt. Stark, KS: De Young, 1997.

Wilford, John Noble. "Discovery Suggests Humans Are Part Neanderthal." *New York Times*. April 25, 1999: 1, 22.

_____. "Skull May Alter Experts' View of Human Descent's Branches." *New York Times*. March 22, 2001: A.1, 10.

Wills, Christopher. *The Runaway Brain: The Evolution of Human Uniqueness*. New York: HarperCollins, 1993.

Wilson, Edward O. *The Insect Societies*. Cambridge, MA: Harvard University Press, 1972.

Wolpoff, Milford H. "Multiregional Evolution: The Fossil Alternative to Eden." In

The Human Revolution: Behavioural and Biological Perspectives on the Origins of Modern Humans. Ed. P. A. Mellars and C. B. Stringer. Edinburgh: Edinburgh University Press, 1989. 62–108.

_____, and A. Thorne. "The Case Against Eve." *New Scientist* (June 22, 1991): 37–41.

_____, and Rachel Caspari. *Race and Human Evolution: A Fatal Attraction.* New York: Simon & Schuster, 1997.

Wrangham, Richard W., and Dale Peterson. *Demonic Males.* New York: Houghton-Mifflin, 1996.

Index